BIRDS of IBERIA

ACKNOWLEDGEMENTS

Published in November 1993 by Mirador Publications S.L.

Photographic copyright © 1993 and credits:
  Buckingham, John: 115,174.
  Butler, A.S.: 99, 100.
  Carlson, Kevin: 41, 46, 47, 65, 71, 72, 75, 80/81, 84, 89, 91, 92, 95, 112, 113, 122,
      127, 132, 133, 135, 140, 142, 143, 144, 146, 148, 149, 150, 155, 163, 167, 169, 171,
      176, 177.
  Cottridge, David: 130, 151, 156, 170, 173.
  Demar, Grant: 44, 124, 147, 152.
  Doherty, Paul: 37, 38, 48, 57, 61, 64, 66, 73, 86, 90, 93, 94, 118, 120, 128, 129,
      139, 145, 153.
  Finlayson, Clive: 8, 16, 18, 19, 21, 22, 23, 24, 25, 27, 28, 29, 30, 31, 50, 51, 54,
      62, 70, 76, 82, 98, 116.
  Green, Dennis: 39, 77.
  Janes, E.A.: 96.
  Kjaer, David: 101, 110, 137, 138, 159, 161.
  Knights, Chris: 158.
  Langsbury, Gordon: 3, 40, 42, 51, 52, 83, 88, 97, 102, 103, 108, 141, 154, 172.
  Nicholls, Howard: 86.
  Peach, A.N.H.: 157.
  Roberts, J. Lawton: 43, 45, 49, 50, 74, 109, 111, 114, 117, 123, 125, 160, 164,
      165, 166, 168, 175, 178.
  Rodríguez, Jose Luis: 78, 79, 105.
  Tidman, Roger: 53, 54, 59, 68.
  Tipling, David: 58, 60, 69, 85, 116.
  Tomlinson, David: 54, 56, 119, 126, 131, 134, 136, 162.
  Woodcock, Martin: 67.

Line illustrations by Alberto Vega Perez.

Graphic design and typography by Bruce Williams, Mijas Pueblo.

Printed by Gráficas San Pancracio, S.L., Pol. San Luis. C/. Orotova 17, Málaga.

ISBN: 84-88127-08-1   Depósito Legal: MA-1.195/1993

BIRDS of IBERIA

by
Clive Finlayson
and
David Tomlinson

 Published by Mirador Books

To Geraldine and Jan

CONTENTS

FOREWORD

When Guy Mountfort's evocative book, Portrait of a Wilderness, was published in 1958, it created tremendous interest among British birdwatchers, attracted by the ornithological treasures of southern Spain. At that time, the package holiday was in its infancy, and for many readers the possibility of visiting the fabled Coto Doñana was no more than a dream.

Today, everything has changed. It costs no more, and takes less time, to fly from London to Málaga than to catch the train from London to Edinburgh. Birdwatching in Iberia is within the reach of every Briton. As a result, many thousands of British birdwatchers have enjoyed watching Lammergeiers over Riglos, Great Bustards in Extremadura, and Bee-eaters in the Algarve. However, despite the interest in Spanish and Portuguese birding, there have been remarkably few books published in English on birds, and birdwatching, in these two countries. Despite its rather grand title, this book does not aim to be the last word on the subject - it would be presumptuous for an Englishman and a Gibraltarian to produce such a work. This volume is simply a guide which aims to inform the reader about the status and distribution of birds in Iberia, with a few clues as to where and when to look for certain species. The background chapters should help to set the scene, and explain why the Iberian peninsula is of such special importance for so many species of birds not found elsewhere in Europe.

It is not intended as a field guide - there are many excellent field guides which can be used in conjunction with this volume as aids for identification. What we do hope is that this volume will encourage more and more people to appreciate the extraordinarily rich and varied birdlife of Iberia, and the importance of conserving the birds, and the landscape, for future generations to enjoy.

Bird populations are constantly changing, so in order to ensure that future editions are as up to date as possible, the authors would be delighted to hear from observers with any information which might be relevant. Please write to Clive Finlayson at the Gibraltar Museum, P.O. Box 939, Gibraltar.

INTRODUCTION

The large peninsula at the southwestern extreme of the continent of Europe - Iberia - began to attract the interest of naturalists during the eighteenth century, a trend started in the 1770s with the Reverend John White, brother of Gilbert White of Selborne. At that time the Reverend White was based in Gibraltar, where he used his spare time exploring and investigating the natural history of the Rock of Gibraltar and its neighbourhood. He wrote a *Fauna calpensis*, a natural history of Calpe - the Phoenician name for Gibraltar. Sadly, the manuscript was lost and only the introduction survives.

We also get an inkling of White's impressions and observations from his letters to his brother Gilbert. The observations of his brother in Andalucía were of great importance in support of those who favoured the view that birds migrated away from northern latitudes in teh autumn.

The tradition had been established. In 1704 the small colony of Gibraltar was captured by a joint Anglo-Dutch force on behalf of Charles of Austria - the pretender to the Spanish throne. It was ceded to Great Britain in 1713 by the Treaty of Utrecht and became a base for the exploration of southern Iberia by British explorer-naturalists. Much of this was to take place in the nineteenth century, a time of

intense activity associated with tfeh expanding British Empire and with changing views about the natural world. The poorer European nations, such as Spain and Portugal, immersed in their own internal politics, lagged far behind in the study of nature.

The presence of a British colony at the apex of a country rich in fauna and flora meant a foothold for its exploration. The tradition therefore developed in close association with the military class - officers stationed on the Rock with sufficient time to devote to exploring and collecting.

The most famous among these was Lt. Col. Howard Irby, who published *The Ornithology of the Straits of Gibraltar* in 1875, followed by a revised and enlarged edition in 1895. Irby explored the "hinterland" of Gibraltar extensively, reaching as far north as the Coto Doñana, making known to the outside world such jewels as the Laguna de la Janda.

The intrepid Willoughby Verner, another officer based in Gibraltar, followed in Irby's footsteps. He wrote *My Life among the wild birds in Spain* in 1910, a vivid account of the countryside of southern Spain and beyond. At about the same time, Abel Chapman and Walter Buck set out to explore southern and western Spain from a nearby, but quite different, base - Jerez at the heart of the sherry-producing country. These early explorers made Iberia, and its ornithological value, known to the outside world and left us a permanent and accurate record of the avifauna of the time.

Iberia suffered its greatest ornithological losses during the twentieth century - ironically when ornithology became best known to outsiders and many naturalists visited Iberia and wrote about it. The Reverend F.C.R. Jourdain, Admiral Lynes and many others contributed to the knowledge of the ornithology of the peninsula. Sadly, there was little local input. It was a time for expeditions.

Atkinson visited southern Spain in the 1930s and wrote *A quest for the Griffon*, a personal acount of more than the Griffons of Cadiz Province or indeed of ts birds. Yeates visited the Coto Doñana later and gave us one of the last accounts of the Laguna de La Janda in his book *Bird Life in two Deltas*.

The most significant of the twentieth century expeditions were those to the Coto Doñana in the late-1950s, vividly presented in Guy Mountfort's *Portrait of a Wilderness*, which led to the eventual protection of Europe's foremost nature reserve.

By the time all this was taking place, Iberian ornithologists had started to emerge. Most notable among these was Tono Valverde, a prime mover of the Doñana protection campaign and the park's first director. Along with Valverde, Francisco Bernis in Madrid became another influential figure in the ornithological world. Bernis was instrumental in the development of the Spanish Ornithological Society (SEO) and became a world authority on Iberian migration and the White Stork. His works included the series *Aves migradoras ibericas* and, towards the end of his career, *La migracion de aves por el estrecho de Gibraltar; Volumen 1.*

The late-1950s and the 1960s saw the upsurge of Palaearctic-African migration studies, led by the monumental works of Reg Moreau. Moreau visited Iberia as part of his studies, as did many other foreign ornithologists with a similar purpose. However, it was in the 1970s that the Iberian ornithological movement took off and research groups were formed in association with universitites and other institutions. The University of Madrid, led by Bernis, developed an important

school and another arose in connection with Doñana. Today, important ornithological research is published from a number of Spanish centres.

On a smaller scale, Gibraltar produced its own Ornithological Society during the 1970s, completing the circle initiated two centuries earlier by John White: on this occasion Gibraltar had produced a group run by the local inhabitants of the tiny peninsula, a reflection of events across Iberia.

Another important development in Iberia during the 1970s and 1980s was the increasing and widespread awareness and concern for the environment. Many environmental protection associations were established across the peninsula, complementing the growth in scientific ornithology. The result is an Iberia which is increasing its protection measures and the surface area of protected land; a Mediterranean peninsula which is beginning to take the lead in ecological protection, thereby changing ingrained attitudes towards wildlife. Portugal has a system of national and natural parks and nature reserves. It has ratified the Ramsar Convention on the protection of wetlands, the Berne Convention on the protection of wildlife habitats and the Bonn Convention which protects migratory birds. Spain and Gibraltar have done likewise. The three are members of the European Economic Community (EEC) and are bound by the Wild Birds directive. The exception is Andorra, which is not in the EEC and which has not ratified the conventions.

So, is Iberia still important for birds and, if so, why? The answer is 'yes' because, despite great losses in habitat and species during the last 80 years in particular, Iberia is still a large peninsula with a great range of climates and topography. With this variety comes a high diversity of wildlife which, in ornithological terms, is further enhanced by the peninsula's strategic position in relation to the major movements of birds in the western Palaearctic.

The following chapters describe the main regions of Iberia, its main habitats and important bird species, as well as its importance to migration. There is then an account of the main species likely to be of interest to the visitor to Iberia, followed by notes on the remaining species.

GEOGRAPHIC REGIONS AND AREAS

FRANCE

ANDORRA

GALICIA
- La Coruña
- Lugo
- Pontevedra
- Orense

ASTURIAS
- Oviedo

CANTABRIA
- Santander

PAIS VASCO
- Bilbao
- San Sebastián
- Vitoria

NAVARRA
- Pamplona

CATALUÑA
- Huesca
- Gerona
- Lérida
- Barcelona
- Tarragona

CASTILLA Y LEON
- León
- Burgos
- Logrono
- LA RIOJA
- Zamora
- Valladolid

ARAGON
- Zaragoza

PORTUGAL

- Salamanca
- Segovia
- Avila
- Madrid
- Guadalajara
- MADRID
- Toledo
- Teruel
- Cuénca

VALENCIA
- Castellón de la Plana
- Valencia

MENORCA

MALLORCA

BALEARIC ISLANDS

IBIZA

EXTREMADURA
- Cáceres
- Badajoz

CASTILLA–LA MANCHA
- Cuidad Real
- Albacete

- Alicante

- Murcia
- MURCIA

ANDALUCIA
- Córdoba
- Sevilla
- Huelva
- Jaén
- Granada
- Almería
- Málaga
- Cádiz

GIBRALTAR
- Ceuta

- Lisbon

MAROCCO

© 1993 BRUCE WILLIAMS

THE REGIONS OF SPAIN

Spain is characterised by a great variety of landscapes in which mountains take up over one third of the territory. In the north the Pyrenees, which stretch from the Bay of Biscay to the shores of the Mediterranean, effectively isolate Iberia from the rest of Europe. Westwards along the northern coast of Spain the Cantabrian mountains dominate the landscape, turning southwestwards in Galicia towards the Portuguese border. The western Cantabrians separate Galicia from central Spain.

The mountains of the Sistema Ibérico run southeastwards from almost the foothills of the western Pyrenees to the Mediterranean coast of Valencia. Here, they come close to the Penibaetic range which arches southwestwards, often close to the coast, to reach the shores of the Strait of Gibraltar. The large Andalucian region is itself isolated from central Spain by the long range known as the Sierra Morena which runs from the Portuguese border to the northeastern tip of Andalucía. The central tablelands of Spain are separated into the northern and southern mesetas by the mountains of the Sistema Central.

Several large rivers are prominent. The Ebro flows southeastwards between the Pyrenees and the Sistema Ibérico to reach the Mediterranean Sea between Cataluña and the Pais Valenciano. Its valley forms a large and arid depression which is locked in by these mountains and by the Cordillera Catalana inthe northeast. The Duero and the Tajo flow westwards across the northern and southern mesetas respectively and reach the Atlantic along the Portuguese coast. Further south the Guadalquivir flows southwestwards between the Penibaetic range and the Sierra Morena to reach the Atlantic at the Coto Doñana.

The following account describes the main features of ornithological interest of each of the autonomous regions of Spain. Areas of particular ornithological importance are highlighted.

ARAGÓN

The large northern region of Aragón is rich and varied for breeding species, combining the mountainous country of the Pyrenees with the arid steppe landscapes of the Ebro, sandwiched between the Pyrenees and the Catalonian ranges in the north and west and the Iberian range in the southeast.

Pyrenees

Some of the most important areas of the Pyrenees are to be found in Aragón. These include mountainous areas with limestone cliffs and crags where Lammergeiers still have an Iberian stronghold. Other cliff nesting species of the area include Griffon Vulture, Egyptian Vulture, Golden Eagle, Bonelli's Eagle, Peregrine Falcon, Eagle Owl, Chough and Alpine Chough. The ranges show the typical transition from alpine grasslands in the peaks, to wooded valleys dominated by beech (*Fagus sylvatica*), oak (*Quercus faginea* and *Q.rotundifolia*), pine (*Pinus sylvestris* and *P.uncinata*) and fir (*Abies alba*) with areas of scrub.

Mammals of these mountains include Spanish Ibex, Chamois and Brown Bear. The woodlands are important for several species which are characteristic of northern Iberia: Capercaillie, Grey Partridge, Black Woodpecker, White-backed Woodpecker and Tengmalm's Owl. Other important woodland species are Red Kite, Honey Buzzard, Booted Eagle and Short--toed Eagle. On the higher ground typical species are Snow Finch, Ring Ouzel and Alpine Accentor.

The most important sites are: (1) Belagua, Anso, Hecho (partly in Navarra); (2) Collarda; (3) Panticosa, Vinamala, Tendenera; (4) Ordesa, Bielsa; (4) Gistain, Cotiella; (5) Posets, La Madaleta, Entecada (partly in Cataluña); (6) San Juan de La Peña, Peña Oroel; (7) Santo Domingo, Riglos, Gratal; (8) Sierra de Guara; (9) Oturia, Cancias; (10) Turbon, Espes, Sis; and (11) Sierras del Montesch y Mongay (partly in Cataluña).

In addition to these sites the Embalse (reservoir) de Tormos in the Pyrenean foothills is an important stopover for migrating Cranes in the spring where up to 7,200 have been counted. Many of the valleys and mountain passes of the Pyrenees are also used by migrating raptors, doves and passerines from where migration can be observed.

Ebro Depression

The arid landscapes of steppe in the interior of the Ebro Valley hold important bird communities with some very interesting species. The higher ground within the depression includes areas which are wooded (e g pine *P.halepensis*, oak *Q.rotundifolia* and juniper *Juniperus thurifera*) or covered in scrub with cliffs and gullies.

The main steppe species are Dupont's Lark, Lesser Short-toed Lark, Stone Curlew, Pin-tailed Sandgrouse, Black-bellied Sandgrouse, Great Bustard (few left), Little Bustard, Montagu's Harrier and Lesser Kestrel. There is a small population of Lesser Grey Shrike in Almacelles-Gimenells between Aragón and Cataluña. Woodland and cliff species include Golden Eagle, Booted Eagle, Short-toed Eagle, Black Kite, Egyptian Vulture and Eagle Owl.

The most important sites are: (1) Montes de Zuera; (2) Sierra de Alcubierre; (3) Bajo Alcandre; (4) El Saso; (5) Los Monegros; (6) Ballobar; (7) Almacelles, Gimenells (partly in Cataluña); (8) Sierra de Valdurrios; (9) Urrea de Jalon; (10) Bajo Huerva; and (11) Belchite.

Gallocanta in southwest Aragón is a large brackish, endorreic, lagoon which is important for migrating Cranes in spring and autumn (with counts of over 22,000 in autumn). It is also an important wintering lagoon for waterfowl, including Red-crested Pochard. Downstream from Zaragoza the Ebro retains small patches of marshy vegetation which are still used for breeding by aquatic species such as Bittern, Little Bittern, Night Heron, Little Egret and Purple Heron. To the southwest of this site the Embalse de Caspe holds Spain's largest Night Heron colony, estimated at 250 pairs.

Iberian Range

The mountains of the Iberian Range cut across the eastern and southern sectors of Aragón. They provide a varied landscape of flat, high ground covered in scrub and crops, limestone cliffs, woodland (*Q.rotundifolia*, *Q.pyrenaica*, *P.pinaster*, *P.nigra*, *P.sylvestris* and *P.halepensis*), scrub, cultivated land and pastures. Steppe and cliff species, typical of the other areas of Aragón, are also found here. The isolated Sierra del Moncayo on the border with Castilla y León has patches of relict woodland and is important for breeding Honey Buzzard, Griffon Vulture, Golden Eagle, Eagle Owl, Grey Partridge, Woodcock, Chough and Alpine Swift.

CATALUÑA

East of Aragón, the northeasternmost region of Spain, Cataluña, provides a range of contrasting habitats and climates. The northern portion of the region includes the eastern end of the Pyrenean chain. Southwards the Catalan Cordillera separates the Ebro Depression to the east from the Mediterranean coastal belt in the west. The Ebro enters the Mediterranean in the southeast of the region, forming a large delta which is of great ornithological significance.

Pyrenees

The eastern Pyrenees has similar characteristics to the central (Aragonese) part and includes some of the best nature reserves. The habitats are, in general, those of the central Pyrenees as are the bird species. These include Lammergeier, Honey Buzzard, Ptarmigan, Capercaillie, Grey Partridge, Black

Woodpecker, Alpine Chough, Tengmalm's Owl and, sporadically, Dotterel.

The main sites are: (1) San Mauricio, Aigues Tortes (regarded as the best site for Capercaillie in the Spanish Pyrenees); (2) Monteixo, L'Orri, Tornafort; (3) Cerdana; (4) Fresser, Setcases; (5) Sierra de Sant Gervas; (6) Sierra de Boumort; and (7) Sierra de Cadi.

Mediterranean Coast

Much of the coastal strip is developed. The best example of Mediterranean vegetation is in the low coastal range in the northeastern province of Girona, between Cap Creus and Golfo de Rosas. This area is characterised by Mediterranean scrub with some oak (*Q.suber* and *Q.rotundifolia*) woods with the important saltmarsh of Aiguamolls de L'Emporda where Bittern and Garganey breed along with other waterbirds. The area is also the Iberian stronghold of the Lesser Grey Shrike.

To the south the small offshore islets known as Islas Medas off Cap Estartit, hold breeding seabirds including Storm Petrel and Shag, as well as the only nesting pairs of Cormorant in Spain.

The most important site on the coastal belt lies right at the south. Here the Ebro opens into the Mediterranean and deposits sediments which form the Ebro Delta, which is said to have formed in the last 1,500 years following intensive upstream erosion since Roman times. The delta includes shallow lagoons, saltmarsh, dunes and beaches as well as paddyfields. It is important for waders, gulls and waterbirds throughout the year. Breeding species include Red-crested Pochard, Black-winged Stilt, Avocet, Collared Pratincole, Slender-billed Gull (the largest Spanish colony), Audouin's Gull (also the largest Spanish colony), Gull-billed Tern, Whiskered Tern, Lesser Crested Tern (occasional), Little Bittern, Squacco Heron and Purple Heron. Wintering species include large numbers of Wigeon, Teal and Shoveler, as well as Greater Flamingo.

Other areas

The Catalan Cordillera, which runs northeast to southwest inland is of interest in that it holds some of the typical breeding species of mountain areas including Golden Eagle, Bonelli's Eagle and Eagle Owl.

The area around Cogull and Alfes in western Cataluña, close to Aragón, has good steppe habitat with typical species including Dupont's Lark, Black-bellied Sandgrouse and Lesser Grey Shrike.

NAVARRA

Navarra is a northern mountain region which includes the western Pyrenees which are gentler than the central and eastern sectors. The breeding species include Lammergeier, Black Woodpecker and White--backed Woodpecker. The latter two species form part of a rich breeding community of woodland (*F.sylvatica, A.alba*) birds in Roncesvalles and Irati. Other important Pyrenean sites are the Sierras de Leyre, Orba and Illón.

In the south the Ebro flows southeastwards and there are areas of steppe habitat which are a continuation of those of the Ebro Valley downstream in Aragón and Cataluña. The area of Bardenas Reales has good breeding populations of Black-bellied and Pin-tailed Sandgrouse, Dupont's and Lesser Short-toed Lark, Great and Little Bustard and Stone Curlew. In the east and southeast of Pamplona, small mountain ranges with limestone cliffs, oak (*Q.faginea*) and beech (*F.sylvatica*) woods and scrub, hold typical mountain breeding birds, such as Egyptian Vulture, Griffon Vulture, Golden Eagle, Bonelli's Eagle and Eagle Owl.

EUSKADI

The Basque country lies in a transition zone between the Pyrenees in the east and the Cantabrian Range in the west. The coastal belt is heavily industrialised but waders and other waterbirds utilise the scattered estuaries on passage, among which the most noteworthy is the estuary of the Guernica river, whose mudflats and marshes are used by waders and Spoonbills on passage.

The Basque country becomes more mountainous towards the west. The Sierra Salvada on the border with Castilla y León runs for 40 kilometres and reaches an altitude of 1,200 metres being dominated by cliffs, scrub and grassland with some oak, beech and pine woodland. Breeding species include Griffon and Egyptian Vulture, Short-toed Eagle, Peregrine Falcon and Alpine Chough.

CANTABRIA

The south of the region is dominated by the impressive ranges of the Cordillera Cantabrica which run east to west parallel to the coastline inland. The coastal belt, which continues westwards from Euskadi, has a number of estuaries and mudflats of which the most important is Santoña, a 2,000 hectare coastal marsh where several estuaries open to the sea. The area is principally important for passage and wintering waders and ducks, and is regarded as northern Spain's best site for Spoonbills on passage.

Inland, the mountain ranges, especially in the southwest, reach altitudes of 2,500 metres and have large limestone cliffs and woods of oak (*Q.robur, Q.pyrenaica, Q.petraea*) and beech (*F.sylvatica*). Wolf and Brown Bear are found in the least disturbed areas. Typical breeding birds are Capercaillie, Grey Partridge, Griffon Vulture, Golden Eagle and Short-toed Eagle. Hen Harriers breed in open upland areas. Important sites are: (1) Sierras de Peña Labra y del Cordel and (2) Fuentes Carrionas, both bordering Castilla y León.

ASTURIAS

The Cantabrian Cordillera continues westwards along the south of the Asturian principality. To its north is the Sierra de Cuera, creating a long depression in between. Along the coast, westwards towards Galicia, the typical shallow estuaries (<u>rias</u>), begin to appear.

Cantabrian Mountains

The main element of Asturian natural history are the mountains in the south which retain a unique mammalian fauna, including Wolf and Brown Bear. These mountains reach altitudes of up to 2,200 metres, and even higher (up to 2,648 metres) in the Picos de Europa in the east. The mountains are characterised by extensive woodland dominated by oaks (*Q.robur, Q.pyrenaica, Q.petraea*), beech (*F.sylvatica*) and birch (*Betula celtiberica*) with scrub and grasslands, and rocks and cliffs higher up. The most important birds are therefore those of woodland and scrub, in particular Capercaillie, Grey Partridge, Black Woodpecker, Middle Spotted Woodpecker and some Short-toed Eagles. The limestone Picos de Europa with high cliffs, gorges, lakes and woods is the most important site in the entire range and has substantial populations of Wall Creeper, Snow Finch, Chough and Alpine Chough, Griffon Vulture, Golden Eagle, Peregrine Falcon and Eagle Owl in addition to the woodland species.

The most important Asturian mountain sites are: (1) Piedrafita, San Isidro; (2) Sierras del Crespón y Mermeja; (3) Reres; (4) Riaño; (5) Muniellos; (6) Degana; (7) Somiedo and (8) the Picos de Europa.

Coastal Belt

The Ria de Ribadeo, bordering Galicia, is the most important site being used by passage and wintering waders and ducks, in particular Sanderling and Pintail. The 65-kilometre rocky coastline from Cabo Torres to Cabo Busto, west of Gijón, has breeding populations of Shag and Storm Petrel.

GALICIA

The Cantabrian Cordillera in Galicia gradually curves southwards towards the northern Portuguese border at Sanabria. This chain separates the lowlands of Galicia from the Meseta Norte, the northern tablelands of central Spain. This western end of the Cantabrian Cordillera, in the southeast of Galicia, is important for Wolf and holds populations of Capercaillie, Grey Partridge and raptors.

Coastal Belt

This area is punctuated by numerous shallow inlets and are important for passage and wintering waders, ducks and seabirds. The coastline is rocky and rugged with scattered offshore islands which are important for breeding seabirds, in particular Shag, Yellow-legged Gull, Lesser black-backed Gull, Kittiwake and Guillemot. The coast, especially around Finisterre, is good for observing seabird migration.

Important seabird breeding sites are: (1) Islas Cies; (2) Islas Ons y Onza; (3) Cabo Finisterre coastline; (4) Cabo Vilan; and (5) Islas Sisargas.

LA RIOJA

The upper course of the Ebro separates this small province from Navarra in the north. Much of the province is taken up by mountains of the northern Iberian Range (Sistema Ibérico), which in some places are deforested and dominated by scrub and grasslands, but in others retain woods of oak (*Q.pyrenaica* and *Q.rotundifolia*), beech (*F.sylvatica*) and pine (*P.sylvestris*). There are also limestone cliffs which are frequented by raptors.

Typical breeding species of these mountains

are Honey Buzzard, Short-toed Eagle, Hen Harrier, Booted Eagle, Bonelli's Eagle, Golden Eagle, Griffon Vulture, Egyptian Vulture, Peregrine Falcon, Eagle Owl, Grey Partridge, Woodcock, Tree Creeper and Marsh Tit. As with the Pyrenees some mountain passes are important for pigeon and passerine migration.

CASTILLA Y LEÓN
Much of this area is taken up by the northern tablelands bisected by the River Duero, which flows from east to west towards the Portuguese border. The vast tablelands are arid and covered by grasslands, heath and cultivation (mostly cereal). Along the Duero some sites are important for waterbirds (e.g. Night Heron) and the river has, in places, cut impressive granite cliffs used by cliff nesting species. These include Egyptian and Griffon Vulture, Golden Eagle, Bonelli's Eagle, Peregrine Falcon, Eagle Owl, Black Stork and Chough.

This is a very large region bordered by mountains in the north and northwest (Cantabrian Mountains), northeast (Sistema Ibérico) and south and southeast (Sistema Central).

Tablelands
These dominate much of the central part of Castilla y León and are largely grasslands, often taken over to cereal cultivation and sheep grazing. Some areas are dotted with pine woods (*P.pinea*). These areas are among the most important in Spain for steppe breeding birds in particular Montagu's Harrier, Great Bustard, Little Bustard, Pin-tailed Sandgrouse, Black-bellied Sandgrouse and Stone Curlew. Dupont's Lark can be found in steppe areas in the northeast and southeast (e.g. at Páramo de Masa and Montejo de la Vega). The Altos de Barahona in the southeast has Spain's most important Dupont's Lark population, with an estimated minimum of 2,000 to 3,000 pairs.

Other important sites are: (1) Los Oteros; (2) Tierra de Campos; (3) Vilafafila; (4) Villapando, Villadefrades; (5) Tordesillas; (6) Alaejos; (7) Madrigal; (8) Gallegos del Pan and (9) Peleas de Abajo.

Sistema Central
The mountains of the Sistema Central, which run in a northeast to southwest direction along the southern edge of Castilla y León are covered in oak

(*Q.rotundifolia, Q.pyrenaica*) with some chestnut (*Castanea sativa*) and pine (*P.sylvestris*) woodland and scrub with some rocky areas. The higher peaks (e.g. at Gredos) have alpine grassland with breeding Bluethroat, Alpine Accentor and Water Pipit. Typical breeding species are Black Vulture, Griffon Vulture, Golden Eagle, Imperial Eagle, Booted Eagle, Bonelli's Eagle, Honey Buzzard, Black Kite, Red Kite and Black Stork. Important sites are: (1) Peña de Francia; (2) Sierra de Gredos; (3) Sierra de Gata (all partly in Extremadura and the latter isolated from the central system at its western end); (4) El Escorial; (5) Sierra de Guadarrama and (6) Sierra de Ayllon (these are partly in the Comunidad de Madrid and/or Castilla-La Mancha).

COMUNIDAD DE MADRID

The small region is sandwiched by the two large regions of Castilla y León (Old Castille) and Castilla-La Mancha (New Castille), and has within it the southern sectors of the Sistema Central in the north (see also Castilla y León) and the valleys of the Manzanares and Jarama (tributaries of the Tagus) in the southeast. Plains in the southeast hold breeding Great and Little Bustard, Stone Curlew and Montagu's Harrier.

The typical breeding species of the Sistema Central breed within the region, including Black Vulture, Imperial Eagle, and Eagle Owl. In addition to the sites described earlier, El Pardo is another important mountain zone.

CASTILLA-LA MANCHA

The southern tablelands, between the Sistema Central in the north and the Sierra Morena in the south and traversed from east to west by the Tajo River, form a vast area of arid lands now largely devoted to wheat growing and wine production. It is the land of Don Quixote. The Tajo rises in the northeast of the region, in the mountains of Guadalajara, part of the Sistema Ibérico, and flows westwards towards Portugal along the northern part of the region. To the south lies the isolated range of the Montes de Toledo. South again the Guadiana River flows westwards towards Portugal to then turn south to reach the sea

along the Andalucian-Portuguese border in the Gulf of Cádiz.

Mountains

In the northeast, the Tajo carves its way through limestone mountains with cliffs, pine woodland (*P.halepensis, P.nigra* and *P.sylvestris*) and scrub. Raptors typical of such areas (e.g. Golden Eagle, Bonelli's Eagle, Egyptian Vulture, Griffon Vulture, Peregrine Falcon and Eagle Owl) are found here. The pattern is similar in the east (Serranía de Cuenca) and southeast in association with the Segura and Mundo rivers. The mountains of the west and southwest are different consisting of scrub covered slopes and oak (*Q.suber, Q.faginea, Q.rotundifolia, Q.pyrenaica*) woods with grasslands and dehesas lower down. This countryside, of which the Montes de Toledo are characteristic, is a stronghold of the Spanish Lynx, raptors (Black Vulture, Imperial Eagle, Golden Eagle, Eagle Owl) and Black Stork. A few pairs of Black-shouldered Kite breed in the southern plains of the Montes de Toledo.

Plains

Wide plains devoted to cereals and some grasslands dominate much of the lowland landscape of the region. It is country which is suited for open ground nesting species of which the most significant are Great Bustard, Little Bustard, Stone Curlew, Black-bellied Sandgrouse, Pin-tailed Sandgrouse, White Stork, Dupont's Lark and Spanish Sparrow. In the southwest the valley and Sierra de Alcudia provides a good combination of the mountain and lowland species of the region, including Pin-tailed and Black-bellied Sandgrouse, Montagu's Harrier, Black-shouldered Kite, Imperial and Golden Eagle, and Black Vulture.

There are scattered lagoons, some highly seasonal, and reservoirs in these arid landscapes which naturally concentrate waterfowl. Some are also important for passage Cranes (El Hito, Puebla de Belena, Embalse de Buendía) as they lie between the Laguna de Gallocanta and the main wintering grounds in Extremadura. The lagoon complex, known as Pedro Muñoz-Manjavacas in the centre of the region has a rich breeding community including Marsh Harrier, Black-necked Grebe, Collared Pratincole, Avocet, Black-winged Stilt and Gull-billed Tern. Other important lagoons for breeding waterbirds are: (1) Dehesa de Monreal; (2) Alcázar de San Juan-Quero complex (including Night Heron and Red-crested Pochard); (3) Tablas de Daimiel (including Little Bittern and Purple Heron and a very large wintering population of ducks); (4) Embalse de Castrejón and (5) Embalse de Azutan.

EXTREMADURA

Extremadura, one of Spain's richest provinces or-
nithologically, lies in the western part of the southern tablelands in the lower courses of the Tajo and
Guadiana rivers before they flow into Portugal.
Extremadura therefore borders with much of central Portugal in the west. It is locked in by mountains to the north (Sistema Central), south (Sierra
Morena in Andalucía) and partly by the Montes de
Toledo in the east. Much of Extremadura is lowland, dominated by steppe and croplands also with
lowland woodland and hills with isolated mountains and rocky outcrops. Dehesas (areas of oak
woodland with large clearings) are typical of many
lowland areas.

Low Sierras, Dehesas and Other Lowland Habitats

Dehesas, dominated by *Q.rotundifolia* but also con-
taining in some areas *Q.suber* and *Q.pyrenaica*, are a
major feature of low, hilly ground which also includes areas of Mediterranean scrub and grassland. Where such areas also contain cliffs, rich
breeding bird communities are found. The mosaic
is completed by areas of steppe and croplands. In
Extremadura many important bird species breed
in such areas and among these the most important
ones are Black-shouldered Kite, Black Kite, Red
Kite, Egyptian Vulture, Griffon Vulture, Black
Vulture, Golden Eagle, Imperial Eagle, Booted
Eagle, Bonelli's Eagle, Montagu's Harrier,
Short-toed Eagle, Peregrine Falcon, Lesser Kestrel,
Eagle Owl, Black Stork, White Stork, Little Bustard,
Great Bustard, Stone Curlew, Collared Pratincole,
Black-bellied Sandgrouse, Pin-tailed Sandgrouse,
Azure-winged Magpie, Great Spotted Cuckoo,
Roller and Spanish Sparrow.

In addition, there are reservoirs which have
nesting colonies of waterbirds, including Night
Heron, Little Egret and large colonies of Cattle
Egret. These areas are also among Spain's most
important wintering areas for Crane and Wood
Pigeon, as well as for some waders (e.g. Lapwing
and Golden Plover). There are many important
sites within this province, among which the following are classed as Important Bird Areas of

Europe (IBA) by the BirdLife International
(Formerly ICBP): (1) Embalse de Gabriel y Galan;
(2) Embalse de Borbollón; (3) Sierra de Coria; (4)
Embalse de Alcantara; (5) Cuatro Lugares; (6)
Monfragüe; (7) Campo Arañuelo; (8) Sierra de las
Villuercas; (9) Embalse de Cijara; (10) Embalse de
Puerto Peña; (11) Sierra de Pela y Embalse de
Orellana; (12) Zorita, Madrigalejo; (13) Trujillo plain;
(14) Trujillo to Caceres plain; (15) Malpartida de
Caceres; (16) Brozas, Membrío; (17) Embalse
de Cedillo; (18) Sierra de San Pedro; (19) Aldea de
Cano, Casas de San Antonio; (20) Embalse del
Salor; (21) Sierra de Montanchez; (22) Lacara; (23)
Mérida area; (24) Botoa, Villar del Rey; (25) El
Membrio, La Albuera; (26) Albala, Malpica;
(27) Cheles, Villanueva del Fresno, Barcarrota; (28)

Dehesas de Jerez de los Caballeros; (29) Fuente de Cantos, Montemolín; (30) Bienvenida, Usagre; (31) Sierra Grande de Hornachos; (32) Granja de Torrehermosa; (33) Peraleda de Zaucejo, Campillo de Llerena; (34) Puerto de Mejoral, Almorchón, Cabeza del Buey; (35) La Serena and (36) Siruela, Agudo.

ANDALUCIA

The southern part of Spain is taken up by the large region of Andalucía. This is arguably Spain's richest ornithological region, mainly because of its geographical situation and its diverse topography. The long chain of rolling mountains (Sierra Morena), which run from the Portuguese border in the west to the northeast of the region, separate Andalucía from the rest of Spain. In the northeast they meet the impressive chains of the Penibaetic Range which run from here southwestwards to reach the Strait of Gibraltar. This chain includes Spain's highest peak, the Mulhacén (3,482 metres), in the Sierra Nevada.

The other main feature of Andalucía is the valley of the Guadalquivir which springs in the Cazorla mountains in the east of the region and reaches the Atlantic in the Gulf of Cádiz, having created a huge marsh (Marismas del Guadalquivir) in its lower reaches. Southwards towards the Strait of Gibraltar the Atlantic coast consists of long, sandy, beaches backed by dunes. The plain of the Guadalquivir (and that of the smaller Guadalete) include a number of endorreic lagoons of great ornithological value. From the Strait north-eastwards much of the narrow coastal belt of the Mediterranean is developed. The coastal stretch around Almería is least spoilt, especially around the Cabo de Gata, and the area to the northwest (on the lee of the Sierra Nevada) has the lowest annual rainfall in Spain with desert habitats in places. This area contrasts with the Sierra de Grazalema, also within Andalucía, which has Spain's highest rainfall.

Sierra Morena

The Sierra Morena consists largely of rugged mountains with some cliffs and a dense cover of Mediterranean scrub or oak woodland (*Q.suber, Q.rotundifolia*) and olive groves. The dehesa countryside of Extremadura to its north continues in many places into this range. Lynx is found in some areas. The birds of the Sierra Morena include some species typical of Extremadura and which reach their southern breeding areas here. The most important breeding species are Black Stork, Black Vulture, Griffon Vulture, Imperial Eagle, Golden Eagle, Bonelli's Eagle, Eagle Owl, and Great and Little Bustard in steppe habitat.

Important sites are: (1) Picos de Aroche; (2) Sierra Morena de Sevilla; (3) Hornachuelos; (4) La Blazquez, La Granjuela, Fuenteovejuna; (5) Hinojosa del Duque; (6) Sierra Madrona and (7) Aldeaquemada, Danador.

Penibaetic Range

In the northeast, the Sierras de Cazorla y Segura, a Biosphere Reserve between the regions of Andalucia, Castilla-La Mancha and Murcia, stand out as ranges reaching up to 2,400 metres and dominated by spectacular cliffs, large pine woods (*P.halepensis, P.nigra, P.pinaster*) and smaller oak woods (*Q.faginea, Q.rotundifolia*) and scrub. Breeding birds include Griffon Vulture, Golden Eagle, Booted Eagle, Peregrine Falcon, Eagle Owl and Chough.

To the southwest, close to the Mediterranean coast, the Sierra Nevada is the ceiling of the Penibaetic Range with several peaks over 3,000 metres. Areas are deforested and much of the vegetation is dominated by scrub and alpine meadows with some pine (*P.sylvestris, P.pinaster*), oak (*Q.rotundifolia, Q.pyrenaica*) and chestnut (*C.sativa*). Breeding species include Golden Eagle, Bonelli's Eagle, Peregrine Falcon, Eagle Owl, Chough and

Alpine Accentor.

The limestone peaks of the Serranía de Ronda lie west of the Sierra Nevada. These stretch from the Sierra Blanca, just by the coast at Marbella, northwestwards towards the Sierra de las Nieves and its highest peak the Torrecilla (1,919 metres) and further west to the Sierra del Pinar behind the town of Grazalema. The habitats of these mountains are varied and include sheer limestone cliffs, grasslands, scrub and pine (*P.pinaster, P.halepensis*), Spanish Fir (*Abies pinsapo*) and oak (*Q.rotundifolia, Q.suber*) woods. The breeding bird community is rich and includes Golden Eagle, Bonelli's Eagle, Booted Eagle, Short-toed Eagle, Griffon Vulture, Egyptian Vulture, Peregrine Falcon, Eagle Owl, White-rumped Swift, Chough, Blue Rock Thrush

and Rock Thrush, Black Redstart, Black Wheatear, Rock Sparrow and Crossbill.

From southwest of Grazalema to the shores of the Strait of Gibraltar sandstone mountains (Sierra de Aljibe) dominate the landscape. These are characterised by large oak woods (*Q.suber, Q.canariensis, Q.faginea*) with scrub and clearings. Cliffs are smaller than in the limestone (known locally as lajas). The area is rich in breeding birds, including a large population of Griffon Vulture as well as Egyptian Vulture, Bonelli's Eagle, Booted Eagle, Short-toed Eagle, Peregrine Falcon, Eagle Owl and White-rumped Swift.

In addition to these main chains, there are smaller outcrops and mountains associated with these which are important, particularly for breeding raptors. These include: (1) Sierra del Cabo de Gata; (2) Sierra de las Cabras; (3) Sierra de Líjar; (4) Peñon de Zaframagón; (5) Sierra Bermeja; (6) Sierra Crestellina; (7) Sierra de Antequera and Sierras de Tejeda and Almijara.

Coastal Marshes and Salt Pans

The main marsh is that of the Guadalquivir including the associated salt pan complex around Bo-

nanza. Other Atlantic marshes of importance are those around Cádiz Bay and the Odiel Estuary with a scattering of other salt marshes, of lesser importance, right down to the Strait of Gibraltar. On the Mediterranean side the Cabo de Gata salt pans are the most important. The marshes are not only rich in breeding species but are also used by thousands of birds (especially waders and ducks) on passage and in winter. In the Guadalquivir in particular, the coastal marshes are closely connected with areas of coastal sand dunes with pine (*P.pinea*) woods and scrub (e.g. Coto Doñana).

The many breeding species include Imperial Eagle, Black Kite, Red Kite, Booted Eagle, Short-toed Eagle, Marsh Harrier, Peregrine Falcon, Hobby, Long-eared Owl, Scops Owl, Little Egret, Purple Heron, Squacco Heron, Spoonbill, Greater Flamingo, White-headed Duck, Marbled Duck, Crested Coot, Purple Gallinule, Black-winged Stilt, Avocet, Collared Pratincole, Pin-tailed Sandgrouse, Kentish Plover, Slender-billed Gull, Gull-billed Tern, Little Tern, Whiskered Tern, Red-necked Nightjar, Great Spotted Cuckoo, Azure-winged Magpie, Lesser Short-toed Lark and Spectacled Warbler.

Lagoons

There are several important lagoon complexes in the region, notably those in the provinces of Cádiz and Córdoba. These are inland lagoons where waters vary greatly in depth both seasonally and annually. They are rich in breeding birds and hold very large numbers of wildfowl in winter. Breeding species include Marsh Harrier, Purple Heron, Little Bittern, Black-necked Grebe, White-headed Duck (now the western European stronghold), Marbled Teal, Red-crested Pochard, Crested Coot, Purple Gallinule, Black-winged Stilt and Collared Pratincole.

Important sites include: (1) Lagunas de Espera; (2) Lagunas de El Puerto de Santamaría; (3) Laguna de Medina; (4) Lagunas de Puerto Real; (5) Laguna de Adra; (6) Lagunas de Córdoba

The brackish Laguna de Fuente de Piedra is unique in that it holds Spain's largest breeding colony of Greater Flamingoes with up to 12,000 pairs. Other breeding species are Slender-billed Gull and Gull-billed Tern.

Steppe and Cultivated Lowlands

There are several arid areas of Andalucía which hold breeding populations of steppe birds. These birds include Montagu's Harrier, Great and Little Bustard, Stone Curlew, Pin-tailed and Black-bellied Sandgrouse, Roller, Lesser Short-toed Lark, Calandra Lark and Thekla Lark. In the most arid regions, particularly in the steppe and desert areas of the southeast of the region (Almería) breeding species also include Dupont's Lark and Trumpeter Finch.

Important sites are: (1) Topares, El Moral, Puebla de Don Fabrique; (2) Hoya de Baza; (3) Hoya de Guadix; (4) Cabo de Gata Steppe; (5) Campo de Nijar, (6) Desierto de Tabernas; (7) Punta Entinas, Punta del Sabinar; (8) Campiña de Carmona and (9) Campillos.

The site of the old freshwater lagoon of La Janda, northwest of the Strait of Gibraltar, consists of flat croplands with scattered woods of pine (*P.pinea*) and dehesa type oak (*Q.suber*) woodland surrounded by sandstone hills and outcrops of the Aljibe ranges. It remains a rich breeding area for steppe birds including Montagu's Harrier, White Stork, Great and Little Bustard, Stone Curlew and Collared Pratincole. It is an important zone for passage birds and a wintering ground for Crane, Imperial Eagle and Black-winged Kite.

MURCIA

This small region is closed off on the east by the Mediterranean Sea and to the west by the northeasternmost ranges of the Penaebetic chain. The arid steppe of Almería in the south spreads northwards between the two. In such areas (e.g. Cagitan, Armorchon and the Valle del Guadalentin) breeding birds include Montagu's Harrier, Little Bustard, Stone Curlew, Black-bellied and Pin-tailed Sandgrouse and Lesser Short-toed Lark.

Small, rocky islands off the coast of Murcia are important for breeding seabirds, especially Storm Petrel and Cory's Shearwater. The saltwater lagoon in the Mar Menor, also on the Mediterranean coast, is used by ducks, waders and flamingoes on passage and in winter, and by Shelduck and Kentish Plover for breeding.

PAIS VALENCIANO

The coastal provinces between Murcia and Cataluña form the region known as Pais Valenciano. The region is characterised by mountain ranges of the Sistema Ibérico inland, and marshes and lagoons along the coast.

Mountains

These take the form of limestone chains (with altitudes below 1,800 metres), with cliffs and pine (*P.sylvestris, P.halepensis, P.nigra, P.pinaster*) and oak (*Q.rotundifolia, Q.faginea*) woodland and Mediterranean scrub. These mountains hold most of the typical Mediterranean breeding species, including Griffon Vulture, Short-toed Eagle, Golden Eagle, Bonelli's Eagle, Peregrine Falcon, Eagle Owl and Chough.

Wetlands

The large area occupied by the Albufera de Valencia is one of Spain's most important wetlands. This is a large coastal lagoon surrounded by rice fields, and coastal sand dunes and pine (*P.halepensis*) woodland. It is a breeding area for wetland species including Night Heron, Little Egret, Purple Heron, Red-crested Pochard, Black-winged Stilt, Collared Pratincole, Kentish Plover and Common Tern. It is regarded as Spain's third most important area for wintering wildfowl, including thousands of Red-crested Pochards.

Other marshes, lagoons and reservoirs along the coastal stretch are also important for waterbirds and include breeding Marsh Harrier, Shelduck, Marbled Duck, Whiskered and Little Tern, in addition to those listed above. These sites are: (1) Prat de Cabanes; (2) Rio Mijares estuary; (3) Estanys y Marjal de Almenara; (4) Embalse del Hondo; (5) Salinas de Santa Pola and (6) Salinas de la Mata y Torrevieja.

Islas Columbretes

These rocky islands off the mainland coast are important for breeding seabirds, especially Storm Petrel, Cory's Shearwater, Audouin's Gull as well as for Eleonora's Falcon.

LAS ISLAS BALEARES

The most important ornithological feature of this archipelago are the rocky islets and cliffs, which are used by breeding seabirds and raptors. Some of Iberia's most important seabird colonies are situated in these islands. The most important nesting seabird species of these rocky areas are Cory's

Shearwater, Mediterranean Shearwater, Storm Petrel, Shag and Audouin's Gull. Breeding raptors include Osprey and Eleonora's Falcon. Black Vulture breeds in the northwest of Mallorca.

The main sites are: (1) Islas Vedra and Vedranell; (2) Cabo Nono and Isla Murada; (3) Isla de Tagomago; (4) Islas de los Freus; (5) La Mola de Formentera; (5) Isla Dragonera; (6) cliffs of northwest Mallorca; (7) Cabo Pinar; (8) Cabo del Freu and Cabo Farruch; (9) Cabo de's Pina; (10) Cap Enderrocat and Cala Pi; (11) Islas Malgrats and Isla de Sech; (12) the northern coast of Menorca and, probably the most important of all, the Cabrera archipelago.

Also of importance in the archipelago is the coastal lagoon in the north of Mallorca known as the Albufera de Alcudia. Breeding species include

Moustached Warbler, Little Bittern and Purple Heron.

PORTUGAL
Mountains

The southwestern extensions of the Cantabrian mountains penetrate the northeast of Portugal. These mountains, north of the Douro River, reach altitudes of up to 1,500 metres and are covered in oak (*Q.robur, Q.pyrenaica*), Chestnut (*C.sativa*) and pine (*P.pinaster, P.sylvestris*) woodland; south of the Douro the Estrela Mountain is the highest in Portugal reaching 2,000 metres. Typical nesting species of these northern Iberian mountains include Honey Buzzard, Short-toed Eagle, Montagu's and Hen Harrier (in open areas), Golden Eagle, Booted Eagle, Peregrine Falcon, Eagle Owl,

Red-backed Shrike, Tawny Pipit and Ortolan Bunting.

South of these mountains the Douro and Tejo wind their way southwestwards towards the Atlantic. Even further south the Guadiana flows west and then south towards the Gulf of Cádiz. Their valleys, and those of their tributaries, are in places rocky and steep and covered in others in a dense oak woodland (*Q.rotundifolia and Q.suber*). The valleys are rich in breeding birds and these include Black Stork, Black and Red Kites, Griffon and Egyptian Vultures, Short-toed Eagle, Golden, Booted and Bonelli's Eagle, Lesser Kestrel, Eagle Owl, Roller, Red-necked Nightjar and Azure-winged Magpie. The avifauna is thus similar to that of the bordering Spanish lands of Extremadura.

Grasslands, Pastures and Cultivated Land

The eastern areas of the Alentejo region, in central and southeast Portugal bordering Spain, include large, flat grasslands, wheatfields and pasture. They contain typical breeding species of such habitats of western Iberia. These birds include White Stork, Black Kite, Black-shouldered Kite, Montagu's Harrier, Lesser Kestrel, Great and Little Bustard, Stone Curlew, Black-bellied Sandgrouse, Roller, Calandra Lark and wintering Crane.

Wetlands

The coastal areas of Portugal include estuaries and lagoons of importance. Among these are the Ria de Aveiro in the north and the Tejo and Sado estuaries further south. These are characterised by coastal mud-flats with salt marsh, salt pans and reeds. They are used by thousands of waders and ducks on passage and in winter, among which are Avocet, Black-tailed Godwit, Curlew Sandpiper and Grey Plover. Breeding birds include Little Bittern, Purple Heron, Marsh Harrier, Black-winged Stilt, Collared Pratincole, Little Tern, Savi's and Great Reed Warbler. This pattern of species is similar in other wetlands, either coastal lagoons or inland freshwater marshes. Being in a zone of major migration of trans-Saharan migrants in late summer and autumn, these habitats are used by many feeding migrants, such as the reed warblers. Freshwater marshes include Paul de Arzila and Paul de Madriz in the central region and Paul do Boquilobo (includes breeding Night Heron and Squacco Heron) in the west. Coastal lagoons include Santo Andre, Sancha and Faro (the latter includes breeding Purple Gallinule and Collared Pratincole).

Rocky Coastal Areas
The rocky coastal belt in the southwest, including cliffs and islets, has breeding Shag, Bonelli's Eagle and Osprey (the only Iberian mainland breeding site). The most important site is the Berlengas Is-

lands off the central Portuguese coast. Breeding species include Cory's Shearwater, Madeiran Petrel, Shag, Lesser Black-backed Gull and Guillemot.

ANDORRA
This small principality, covering 468 square kilometres of eastern Pyrenees, is important for some of the typical breeding birds of this mountain range. In the woods of pine, fir and oak Capercaillie and Short-toed Eagle breed, along with other mountain species in open areas and cliffs, in particular Ptarmigan and Golden Eagle.

GIBRALTAR
The territory of Gibraltar includes an area of 600 hectares of well-developed maquis dominated by wild olive as well as sheer limestone cliffs. The Rock is an isolated outcrop of the Penibaetic Range. Breeding species include Barbary Partridge (the only site on mainland Europe), Peregrine Falcon, Lesser Kestrel and Blue Rock Thrush. The peninsula is important for many migratory and wintering species including many species of raptor, passerines and seabirds. Among the wintering species are Black Redstart and Chiffchaff.

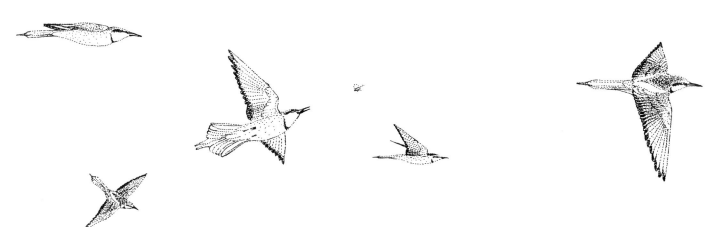

BIRD MIGRATION THROUGH THE IBERIAN PENINSULA

For the student of bird migration, the Iberian Peninsula is a prime hunting ground. Situated in the southwesternmost corner of Europe, it acts as a bridge between Africa and northwestern and central Europe, even western Asia. The Iberian Peninsula sees most of the migrants which travel between northern, western and central Europe and western Africa. Which are these migrants and why do they cross Iberia?

Perhaps the most spectacular of the migrations are those of the soaring birds, raptors and storks. Iberia holds some of the most important breeding populations of raptors of Europe, not just the endangered species like the Spanish Imperial Eagle but of commoner species too. Birds like the Black Kite, the Montagu's Harrier, the Booted Eagle, the Short-toed Eagle or the Egyptian Vulture all have a major European stronghold in Iberia. These birds, along with the 30,000 Spanish White Storks, clearly migrate along specific routes within Iberia. These populations are not the only ones to migrate along the peninsula: many continental raptors (including Honey Buzzards from Scandinavia, Black Kites from Germany and Switzerland and Sparrowhawks from much of central and northern Europe) cross the peninsula during their twice-yearly journeys between the breeding grounds and the winter quarters.

These continental migrants cross the Pyrenees, following mountain passes and valleys from where they can be observed, especially during the southward passage from localities such as Orgambideska. They follow inland and coastal routes to and from the Strait of Gibraltar, concentrating largely over the eastern half of Iberia. The approach of many continental raptors towards the Strait of Gibraltar in summer and autumn is invariably from the Mediterranean coastline to the northeast. In contrast, many Iberian migrants come from the Atlantic coast to the northwest: western and central Iberia are the stronghold of these species, so their approach route differs from that of the continental migrants.

The migrating soaring birds aim to cross between Europe and Africa at the Strait of Gibraltar. Here, the sea-crossing is the shortest in the western Mediterranean -- only 14 kilometres -- which is ideal for birds unable to fly long distances over the sea. Each season 250,000 raptors and over 30,000 storks congregate over the Strait; they attempt to soar over one side and glide to the other. In practice, conditions do not always permit such a smooth passage and often birds struggle to reach the other shore. They also drift with the prevailing winds so that the passage lines can vary across the width of the Strait.

The Iberian Peninsula is also an important zone for the migration of the smaller landbirds, passerines and related groups. Broadly, two types of movements can be recognized in the autumn. The migrants which will cross the Sahara Desert to winter in tropical Africa migrate first, with some species such as the Melodious Warbler migrating as early as July. These birds cross Iberia at the height of the drought and they avoid, to a very large degree, the drier eastern half. Millions of migrants instead aim for the wetter north-west, where birds like the Pied Flycatcher are able to feed and fatten up before the crossing of the Sahara. From there they fly south over Portugal and out to sea from the southern coast of Portugal. This movement takes them to the Atlantic coast of Morocco and they then continue into tropical Africa along the western fringe of the Sahara. The eastern edge of this migratory line appears to be in the region of the Strait of Gibraltar, where trans-Saharan migrants are still visible in large numbers.

This early movement is followed by a later one of birds which will winter in Iberia and Morocco. These birds arrive mainly in October and November, by which time the drought is usually over. They then concentrate along the Mediterranean side of Iberia, some following the coast towards the Strait and into Morocco, others remaining to winter in the milder lowland areas of eastern and southern Spain. For many birds, like Meadow Pip-its, White Wagtails and Blackcaps, the Mediterranean coast of Spain, together with the Strait and the Moroccan lowlands, is a major wintering ground.

In spring it is these migrants which leave first and constitute the main waves of migrants crossing Iberia from southwest to northeast. Already in February there is a pronounced passage of Chiffchaffs, Blackcaps and Song Thrushes among others. March is a main month of passage and one which sees the gradual arrival of the tropical African migrants. These peak during April and May when large movements are seen over Iberia by radar. These birds are reaching the area when insects and other foods are in abundance and they use Iberia to refuel after the long crossing of the Sahara. There is no concentration in the west at this time. In fact, many migrants are heading north-east from Morocco and these continue along central and eastern Spain. This time of year is excellent for large falls along coastal areas of the Strait and the Mediterranean coastline after bad weather. It is not unusual then to come across patches of coastal scrub literally covered in warblers, chats and other migrants.

The Atlantic coastal belt, with its tidal estuaries and mud flats, is the principal zone for the migration of waders. These species utilize these sites on passage to the major wintering grounds off the Atlantic coast of Morocco and the Banc d'Arguin

in Mauretania. Others follow the Mediterranean coast of Iberia, but are more restricted in choice of stop-over sites. The extensive developments along this coast have significantly reduced the availability of resting areas, although some important sites do remain, including the delta of the Ebro river and the salt pans of the Cabo de Gata in the southeast.

Wildfowl movements in Iberia take the form of mass arrivals of birds in autumn which will winter largely within the peninsula. Most noteworthy is the huge concentration of Greylags in the Marismas del Guadalquivir but large numbers of other ducks (e.g. Teal, Shoveler and Wigeon) concentrate in coastal and inland lagoons and marshes, with the Guadalquivir forming the main nucleus of concentration.

Cranes follow a similar pattern of passage, with large autumn and spring movements of birds which will chiefly winter in Iberia. They do so in the west and southwest with a few crossing the Strait of Gibraltar into northwest Africa. The main wintering grounds are in the dehesas of Extremadura. Cranes use traditional stop-overs and the Laguna de Gallocanta is one of the most important transit areas between the wintering grounds and sites north of the Pyrenees.

Seabirds also perform impressive movements along coastal areas of Iberia; the Strait of Gibraltar is probably the best area for observing these movements, as birds moving between Atlantic and Medi-

terranean areas are forced to congregate within the narrow channel. Northeastern Atlantic species follow the Atlantic coastline south in autumn. Some, like Gannets, Puffins and Razorbills move quickly, sometimes out of sight of land. Others, such as Lesser black-backed Gulls, stop along the many Atlantic inlets and estuaries to feed and rest. On reaching the latitude of the Strait many Gannets, Lesser black-backs and Pomarine Skuas continue south towards wintering grounds off West Africa. Others stay in the area for the winter or penetrate into the Mediterranean. Their return movements in spring are equally impressive.

Mediterranean breeding seabirds also use the Strait on passage. In summer and autumn spectacular movements take place of Mediterranean and Cory's Shearwaters, Audouin's Gulls and Lesser Crested Terns. The gulls in particular gather in large flocks on beaches and estuaries. The return movement in February and March is also large.

Seabirds from further east also reach and cross the Strait after passing the length of the Mediterranean or after crossing continental Europe. Among the most abundant migrant seabirds are Sandwich Tern, Black Tern and Mediterranean Gull.

Iberia is in a privileged location for migration of most kinds. Be it soaring birds, waders, passerines or seabirds, the lands of this peninsula offer unique opportunities for the observation of special birds, often in very large concentrations.

WATERBIRDS AND SEABIRDS

BLACK-NECKED GREBE
Zampullín Cuellinegro *Podiceps nigricollis*

This handsome little bird breeds in scattered colonies on eutrophic lakes in southern, central and eastern Spain. Insects and molluscs make up much of its diet, so it favours shallow, highly productive, waters. Where conditions are suitable, colonies of as many as 200 or 300 pairs may flourish, but few of these are stable; changing conditions or even disturbance may cause the site to be deserted. This bird will readily make use of seasonally flooded lakes, and is familiar in parts of Andalucía on lakes draining small towns, where the over-enriched waters produce good feeding.

In the winter it is more widespread, more catholic in choice of habitat, and is frequently found on salt pans and on the sea. One of the largest winter concentrations is on the old salt pans at the northern end of Formentera, where peak counts have been close to 4,000 birds. Similar numbers also occur regularly on the Salinas de la Mata y Torrevieja, near Valencia.

Black-necked Grebe

CORY'S SHEARWATER
Pardela Cenicienta *Calonectris diomedea*
This large, long-winged shearwater is a bird of tropical and warm temperate waters, breeding in the Canaries, Madeira, the Azores and the Balearic Islands, as well as in scattered colonies elsewhere in the Mediterranean. It is a bird that can frequently be seen from suitable sea-watching points around the Mediterranean and western Atlantic coasts of Iberia, often in large numbers. It is best recognized by its size, being the largest of the European shearwaters, and its distinctive, gannet-like, flight with strong wing beats interspersed with long glides on curved wings.

Thousands of birds pass through the Strait of Gibraltar in both spring and autumn, and up to 3,000 an hour have been counted in peak periods. Although Cory's Shearwaters will scavenge from fishing boats, most of their food is caught by plunge-diving.

Like most shearwaters, Cory's only come to their breeding colonies under cover of darkness; they favour uninhabited islands, or steep mountainous terrain, nesting underground. It has been estimated that more than 10,000 pairs nest in the Balearics, Columbretes and Chafarinas Islands; the only mainland colonies in Iberia are on the coast of Portugal, with a mere 100 pairs.

Cory's Shearwater   Right: *Gannet in flight*

MEDITERRANEAN SHEARWATER
Pardela Pichoneta *Puffinus yelkouan*
Until recently the Balearic Shearwater was regarded as a race of the widespread Manx Shearwater, but it has recently been given its own full specific status. It is now classified as forming a super-species with the similar Levantine Shearwater (also once regarded as a race of the Manx), but can be recognized by its darker underside and paler back and wings. Its breeding population in the Balearics, Columbretes and Chafarinas is estimated at between 1,000 and 5,000 pairs, and is generally less numerous than Cory's Shearwater. Small numbers can be seen off Spain's Mediterranean coast throughout the year, though many birds move out into the Atlantic in June, returning early in the New Year.

Levantine Shearwaters can also be seen regularly off Spain's Mediterranean coast, with peak numbers in the Strait of Gibraltar between late June and early September. However, only a few birds are seen in the winter.

GANNET
Alcatraz *Sula bassana*
Although the nearest breeding colonies of Gannets to Iberia are in northwestern France and around the coast of Britain, this species is a common and, at times, abundant visitor to both the Atlantic and Mediterranean coasts of Spain and Portugal. After breeding, the majority of Gannets disperse south along the eastern Atlantic coast, some going as far south as equatorial West Africa. Many of these birds pass close to the Atlantic coasts of Spain and Portugal, while more than 20,000 may pass through the Strait of Gibraltar and winter in the Mediterranean. Gannets do not breed until they are at least five years old, and immature birds frequently remain in southern waters, or within the Mediterranean, for the first year or two of their lives.

SHAG

Cormorán Moñudo *Phalacrocorax aristotelis*

If you see a cormorant-like bird off the coast of Spain or Portugal it is most probably a Shag, as Cormorants are winter visitors but Shags are resident throughout the year. Shags nest on the cliffs of Spain's northern coastline, along the Algarve in Portugal, as well as in the Balearics and on the Rock of Gibraltar. However, numbers are generally small and it is unusual to see more than few birds together. They are very much maritime birds, rarely found inland.

Immature Mediterranean Shags are lighter in colour than the Atlantic birds and can appear notably pale in bright sunshine. The Mediterranean shag is given sub-specific status as *P.a.desmarestii.* The Balearic Islands are particularly important for Shags. The largest colony in the Mediterranean (250 pairs) is on the limestone cliffs of southern Majorca, between Cap Enderrocat and Cala Pí.

LITTLE BITTERN

Avetorillo *Ixobrychus minutus*

Wherever there are suitable reed beds in Iberia there is a chance of finding Little Bitterns for these small, secretive, herons are surprisingly widespread. They favour lush vegetation or reed beds alongside rivers, ponds or lakes, but they are easily overlooked because of their secretive, crepuscular, habits. They are usually seen at dusk, when they are most active, climbing clumsily to the tops of reeds, or flying across patches of open water on jerky wing beats. Although these birds appear to be poor fliers, this is only an illusion; they are highly migratory, moving south into tropical Africa in late August and early September, returning again at the end of March or early April. Some occasionally winter in the south.

One way of locating Little Bitterns is by listening for the male's distinctive spring song, which sounds like a distant, muffled dog bark, and is repeated at two-second intervals. However, they are often found in areas where frog populations are high, and the croaking of several thousand frogs can drown the sound of the Bittern. They are curious birds, sometimes appearing not to notice

Left: *Shag on rock*

Little Bittern

the presence of humans, and allowing the observer to approach within a metre or two before taking to the wing. They rarely feed in the open but can sometimes be watched fishing along the edge of a dyke, stalking slowly in search of amphibians, small fish or even insects.

BLACK-CROWNED NIGHT HERON
Martinete *Nycticorax nycticorax*
Widespread but localised, the Night Heron is easily overlooked and is possibly more numerous than records suggest. Its Iberian stronghold is the Marismas of the Guadalquivir but small numbers nest along many of the major rivers of Spain and

Portugal. It is a nocturnal heron, leaving its roost at dusk in search of feeding areas and often travelling considerable distances in doing so. It is often its loud "quark" call, usually uttered in flight, that gives away the bird's presence as it flies overhead on stiff, rounded, wings.

Night Herons are migratory, returning from their wintering grounds in tropical Africa in March, although some remain in Iberia all winter; most breeding birds return by mid-April. They migrate mainly at night, flying in small groups in straight-line formation. They nest in trees or shrubs, usually in company with other nesting herons. Among the more important Portuguese sites for this species are the freshwater marshes of Paul do

Night Heron

Boquilobo (100 pairs), and the valley of the River Guadiana, in Alentejo (150 pairs).

SQUACCO HERON
Garcilla Cangrejera *Ardeola ralloides*

This small, attractive species, which looks much whiter on the wing than on the ground, is the least numerous of the Iberian herons. It has, however, increased gradually during the present century and there are now at least six, possibly more, colonies with more than 300 breeding pairs. The largest (200 pairs) is within the egretry at La Noria in the Ebro Delta, and is one of the easiest places to see this bird.

This species is another African migrant, return-ing to southern Europe in mid-April. Southward migration starts in late August with the last birds remaining until early October. Occasionally, some remain in winter. Vagrants can occur on almost any wetland but they are most likely to be found on lagoons close to the Mediterranean coast. Occasionally, migrants will be found perched on rocks along the beach.

Squaccos are relatively easy birds to watch for they will feed in the open, particularly early in the morning. They are, however, surprisingly well camouflaged and are easily overlooked until they take off. They are communal birds, building their platform of twigs usually in dense thickets of willow, and in company with other species of herons.

Squacco Heron   Overleaf: *Cattle Egret*, right: *Little Egret*

CATTLE EGRET
Garcilla Bueyera *Bubulcus ibis*

The Cattle Egret is something of an Iberian speciality foruntil 25 years ago it was rarely seen elsewhere in Europe. However, the Spanish population has been slowly expanding its range northwards, leading to the colonization of the Camargue, where it was proved to nest for the first time in 1968. Numbers have grown steadily in the Ebro Delta, which now has around 2,000 breeding pairs. However, its stronghold remains in Andalucía and the Alentejo region of Portugal. Here it is an abundant, familiar bird as likely to be seen feeding around cattle and horses as prospecting in rubbish tips and even ploughed fields. In the evening long lines of Cattle Egrets make their way back from their feeding grounds to their favoured roosts, where thousands of birds may gather together.

Cattle Egrets are partial migrants; many remain on their breeding grounds throughout the year, but others disperse to the south. There is a passage across the Strait of Gibraltar in late August and early September, with a return movement starting in January. Cattle Egrets nest in tight, noisy, colonies often in reed beds or low trees in water, but sometimes in tall trees away from water.

LITTLE EGRET
Garceta Común *Egretta garzetta*

This striking, all-white Egret is slowly expanding its range in western Europe. In Spain and Portugal it is still colonizing new areas, for example, nesting for the first time in Navarra as recently as 1983. It is also increasing in numbers in the south and east; in Valencia, the breeding population doubled from 700 pairs in 1986 to about 1,400 pairs in 1989. Non-breeding birds are also frequently encountered on the estuaries of the northern coast, where this species was once a rarity.

Nesting colonies are scattered throughout northeastern Spain, but it is at its most numerous as a nesting bird in the southwest. However, it is notable that there are now more pairs nesting in the Ebro (600 pairs) than the Marismas del Guadalquivir (400 pairs). The total Iberian population is thought to be around 3,000 pairs, but is now growing quite rapidly.

Non-breeding birds can be encountered anywhere along the Mediterranean coast throughout the year although the majority of birds winter in Africa. This species is seldom found far from water, and though it is not unusual to see solitary birds, it is more often found in small, loose groups. Its strongholds in Iberia may be river estuaries and deltas, but there are also a number of inland breeding colonies and wandering birds will turn up almost anywhere where there is shallow water, suitable for fishing in.

It usually feeds in the open, well away from cover, stalking flooded meadows, rice paddies or salt pans for insects, frogs, crustaceans and fish. It nests in colonies, usually in association with other species of heron.

Purple Heron feeding young

Black Stork at nest

PURPLE HERON
Garza Imperial *Ardea purpurea*

Purple Herons are widespread nesting birds in Iberia, occurring in the south and east wherever suitable habitat can be found. This is a bird which likes well-vegetated, freshwater wetlands, for it seldom feeds far from cover. It occupies sites along many river valleys, and shallow inland lakes (including reservoirs) fringed with reed beds. The largest colonies, with several hundred pairs, are in the Marismas del Guadalquivir but the Ebro also holds up to 300 pairs.

Most often seen as it flies to favoured feeding areas, the Purple Heron is readily identified from the Grey Heron by its more sinuous, snake-like, neck and its dark colouring. Another useful field mark when compared to the Grey Heron is its longer hind claw, making its feet look much bulkier when flying.

Purple Herons winter in sub-Saharan Africa and although the first birds return to Iberia in March, the majority arrive in April with the return passage starting as early as late July. They migrate at night, so it is relatively rare to see passage birds. Like the majority of Iberian herons they nest in colonies, often mixed with other species of herons but sometimes by themselves. Some remain in Iberia in winter.

BLACK STORK

Cigüeña Negra *Ciconia nigra*

The first Black Storks cross the Strait of Gibraltar as early as mid-February on the way back to their breeding grounds. Between 150 and 200 pairs of this shy, secretive, bird nest in Spain with a further 35-50 pairs in Portugal. The Portuguese stronghold is the upper River Douro. Most of the Spanish birds are to be found in Extremadura (the best area is Monfragüe Natural Park), south to northern Andalucía, but the occasional pair will nest well away from the more regular sites. Iberia's Black Stork population has never been properly counted, but it seems likely that it is slightly increasing, rather than decreasing.

Unlike the closely related White Stork, the Black Stork avoids contact with people, nesting on cliff faces or in tall trees, never on buildings. It is also a relatively solitary bird, although two nests in the same tree have been recorded, while it will also nest close to Grey Herons. After breeding, groups will gather together -- flocks of up to 50 birds have been recorded at Zujar Dam, La Serena, Extremadura, and up to 80 birds together on autumn passage across the Strait of Gibraltar.

With such a small population, it can be difficult to locate nesting pairs, especially in the extensive plains of Extremadura. It is best looked for in damp or marshy areas, for it likes to feed in shallow wetlands and will readily fly considerable distances from its nest site to feed.

Although the majority of the population is migratory, moving south into tropical West Africa in September and early October, there are many records of birds remaining in Spain during the winter months.

White Stork

Glossy Ibis

WHITE STORK
Cigüeña Blanca *Ciconia ciconia*

White Storks are among the most familiar, and popular, of Iberian birds; their bulky nests are a familiar site on churches throughout central Spain and eastern Portugal. Sadly, this species has been declining steadily throughout the second half of this century. In 1948, there were an estimated 26,000 pairs in Spain, but this had dropped to 18,500 in 1958, when the Portuguese population was thought to be about 5,500 pairs. Today the Spanish population is estimated at about 7,000 pairs, the Portuguese between 2,000 and 5,000, and the gradual decline continues.

However, in its strongholds, such as the Ebro Valley and in parts of Andalucía and Extremadura, it remains a common bird and some churches boast as many as four or five active nests. In Cataluña there is in existence a reintroduction programme in the Aiguamolls de l'Empordà where birds can be seen stalking the El Matà paddy fields throughout the year (birds that are released lose their migratory instinct). The majority of birds move south to the steppe and savannah zones of the northern tropics.

White Storks start to migrate in late July with the peak passage in August. However, the first returning flocks may appear in mid-November, even late October, with nesting taking place in December. This suggests that the storks move to avoid the dry autumn and return with the winter rains.

GLOSSY IBIS
Morito *Plegadis falcinellus*

The Glossy Ibis is one of Spain's lost breeding birds. It certainly bred from at least 1774 to the early 20th century and there were isolated nesting attempts in 1909, 1930 and 1935. It is now recorded in small numbers on spring and autumn migration in the Balearics, with some birds remaining for several weeks if the feeding is suitable. It remains a scarce migrant to the mainland.Because Glossy Ibises are great wanderers, tracing the origin of the birds recorded in Spain is difficult, although a bird ringed in Hungary has been recovered in Spain.

SPOONBILL
Espátula *Platalea leucorodia*

The Iberian Spoonbill breeding population, estimated between 600 and 700 pairs, is one of the largest in Europe. The majority -- perhaps 350 pairs -- nest in the Coto Doñana, feeding in the Marismas del Guadalquivir. The nearby estuary of the Rio Odiel supports a further 300 pairs but this species is surprisingly scarce, and does not breed, in the Ebro Delta.

Wandering spoonbills can occur anywhere, but the largest numbers of migrants are found on the estuaries of northern Spain. Up to 100 passage birds have been recorded on the estuary of the Ría de Guernica in Euskadi, with smaller numbers on the Marismas de Santoña in Cantabria. These are probably Dutch birds, moving between their breeding grounds in Holland and their wintering areas in West Africa. The Faro Lagoon (next to Faro Airport in the Algarve) is also a regular migration point for these birds, with up to 50 recorded at passage times. The Banc D'Arguin in Mauretania is their probable destination, for up to 4,000 Spoonbills have been recorded there in mid-winter. Many of the Spanish birds also winter in Africa but a considerable number remain close to the breeding areas. Return passage starts early, with the first arrivals in February.

GREATER FLAMINGO
Flamenco *Phoenicopterus ruber*

Flamingoes have been familiar birds in southern Spain for centuries, but they have a chequered history as breeding birds. They have attempted to nest in the Marismas del Guadalquivir on several occasions this century, but generally with little

Left: *Spoonbill with young*   *Greater Flamingoes*

success. However, up to 10,000 birds regularly winter here. Today, the only permanent Spanish colony is at La Laguna de Fuente de Piedra in Malaga, Andalucía, with up to 12,000 pairs. This extensive lake is now an ICONA reserve and is one of Spain's Ramsar sites. The whole area is fenced and, thanks to this lack of disturbance, the flamingoes enjoy considerable breeding success.

As a result, flamingo numbers have built up in Spain and now these spectacular birds are a familiar sight on salt pans and coastal lagoons along the Mediterranean coast. In recent years, there have been a number of breeding attempts at new sites, including the Salinas de Santa Pola, in Valencia. The Ebro delta regularly holds up to 1,000 flamingoes (particularly in summer), many of which are probably non-breeding birds and there is certainly considerable interchange between the French and Spanish populations. Like geese, flamingoes do not breed until they are three years old, so many of the non-breeding birds will be immatures.

GREYLAG GOOSE
Ansar Común *Anser anser*

With a wintering population of up to 70,000 Greylags, the Marismas del Guadalquivir is one of the most important areas in Europe for this species. Ringing has shown that most of the birds which winter here are from Scandinavian and German populations. They leave their breeding grounds in late September and move southwest through the Netherlands and on through France and into Spain. The passage is rapid, some birds following the French coast, others migrating over the Pyrenees. Numbers peak in December and January before the more leisurely return migration begins. They have always been highly valued sporting birds in the Marismas and many are shot.

Small numbers of Greylags do winter away from the Guadalquivir - for example, the Tejo Estuary, regularly holds 400 and in hard winters as many as 800. Elsewhere, Greylags are generally passage migrants, seldom stopping for long.

Left: *Greylag Goose*   *Ferruginous Duck*

FERRUGINOUS DUCK
Porrón Pardo *Aythya nyroca*

This small, dark, diving duck is now probably the rarest breeding duck in Iberia - it may have even been lost as a regular nesting bird altogether. Spain was always on the western limit of its range, which during the past 30 years has contracted eastward. However, the nesting population in the Marismas del Guadalquivir was once estimated at 500 pairs, but whether any remain is doubtful.

Ferruginous Ducks are now increasingly rare vagrants to overgrown freshwater lakes and marshes throughout the country - they are rarely seen on open or exposed waters. Because of their retiring habits they may be overlooked and may occur anywhere. One of the authors of this book once watched a female Ferruginous fly in from the sea to a small freshwater pool on Menorca in early September. It was clearly a tired migrant, allowing a close approach.

Marbled Teal

MARBLED TEAL
Cerceta Pardilla *Marmaronetta angustirostris*
Marbled Teal were one of the commonest ducks in the Marismas of the Guadalquivir, and at the end of the 19th century there were reputed to be several thousand pairs. However, numbers fell sharply in the early years of this century and continued to decline for the next 80 years. Recently, however, numbers have noticeably increased, with nesting recorded from new sites including the Balearics, and in 1991 in Daimiel, Ciudad Real - the first time this species has been found breeding in central Spain.

The reasons for the original decline, or the recent recovery, are not clear. Today, this species' breeding range is very fragmented. Its most important breeding areas are in Iraq and Iran, with smaller numbers in Turkey and Pakistan. Morocco is also an important area where numbers are on the increase.

The Marbled Teal is one of several Iberian breeding birds listed on the ICBP World Check-list of Threatened Birds. Despite the increase, nesting is known from only a few sites. The most northern regular site is the Embalse del Hondo, with up to 15 breeding pairs, but the stronghold is in the Marismas del Guadalquivir where the current breeding population is thought to number between 100 and 200 pairs.

As the Marismas dry out in the autumn so the majority of teal move away, with most moving south to winter in Morocco (where there have been recoveries of Spanish ringed birds). Others disperse to the northeast and there are many records of this species on the Mediterranean coast between Alicante and Valencia - the Albufera de Valencia is probably a good place to watch for this species in autumn, as is the Laguna de Medina, where autumn counts have exceeded 100 birds. There are some records from the Ebro.

Marbled Teal are unusual among European dabbling ducks in that the sexes are identical (apart from the bill, which is all-black in the drake but has a creamy-yellow base in the duck). They are quiet, unobtrusive birds, usually staying close to cover. In flight, they have noticeably slower wing beats than Teal and generally drop down out of sight soon after being flushed. They nest on the ground, but in the Marismas they frequently nest on the grass-thatched roofs of the traditional low guardians' houses.

RUDDY SHELDUCK
Tarro Canelo *Tadorna ferruginea*
This handsome shelduck has always been a rare visitor to southern Spain and although it is generally thought to have been a former nesting bird, there is no proof that it ever bred. It certainly occurred more frequently in the past than it does today, which is a reflection of the severe decline of the North African population - the source of Spanish birds. This bird has not bred in either Algeria or Tunisia for many years while in northern Morocco only a small population survives (probably no more than 50 pairs). However, farther south, in the Atlas, the population is considerably larger.

Earlier this century up to 200 Ruddy Shelduck wintered in the Marismas del Guadalquivir, arriving from August through to October and remaining until the following February or March. Numbers started to decline during the '50s and '60s, and today this species is no more than a rare visitor. There have been attempts to reintroduce this bird to the Coto Doñana but they have not been notably successful.

Occasional migrant Ruddy Shelduck appear on the Mediterranean coast of Spain and there is a scattering of Portuguese records. These certainly refer to post-breeding dispersal of North African birds and is interesting as the only example of a species nesting in Africa migrating north to Europe (but see Royal Tern).

Red-crested Pochard

RED-CRESTED POCHARD
Pato Colorado *Netta rufina*

As many as 6,000 or 7,000 pairs of this handsome, unmistakeable, duck nest in Spain, the majority on the shallow eutrophic lakes in the region of Ciudad Real, a few of which hold several hundred pairs. There are also many sites on the Mediterranean coast where this species breeds, with the largest colony (1,500 breeding pairs) on the Ebro Delta.

Smaller numbers nest in the Marismas del Guadalquivir while Red-crested Pochard will also use man-made lakes if conditions are suitable, such as the Embalase del Hondo (Valencia), which has up to 500 pairs. The preferred habitat is freshwater lakes with extensive reed cover, and preferably with emergent aquatic plants.

In winter several sites can boast quite spectacular gatherings of this species. At Gallocanta, a large brackish lagoon in Aragón, the wintering flock regularly exceeds 8,000 birds when the water conditions are right (this lake may dry up completely); the Albufera de Valencia averages more than 5,000 birds in mid-winter, with peak counts as high as 12,200; and about 5,000 winter in the Marismas del Guadalquivir.

Unlike the Ferruginous Duck, the Red-crested Pochard is currently thriving well in Spain. It apparently nested for the first time in the Marismas del Guadalquivir only 50 years ago, so has gained much ground during this century.

WHITE-HEADED DUCK
Malvasía *Oxyura leucocephala*

Twenty years ago, the White-headed Duck looked set to become extinct in Spain; the population dropped almost to the point of no return, with just a few pairs left in southern Andalucía. Now, thanks to careful protection of several of its favoured lakes, this unusual and interesting bird has staged a major comeback, with a population probably in excess of 350 pairs. This population is sedentary - there is considerable local movement - but most birds are thought to remain within Spain throughout the year.

White-headed Ducks have specialised habitat requirements, which partially explains why their current range is so fragmented. They are invariably found on shallow, open, lakes bordered with dense vegetation. Despite the fact that they find most of their food by diving, they favour water often less than 1 metre deep. They are found exclusively in the warm temperate zone, with the largest population centred around Kazakstan, wintering south to Pakistan. This species is believed to be extinct in Sicily, Sardinia and Corsica, all former strongholds, while the Hungarian population, which died out in the late 1950s, is the subject of a reintroduction scheme.

In Andalucía, the most reliable site to see this species is the Laguna de Medina, close to Jerez. Here, several pairs breed and wintering numbers have recently exceeded 600. The other important site is the complex of brackish lagoons near Aguilar in the south of Córdoba. Most of the lagoons are protected from both hunting and disturbance, for they are within an Integral Reserve of Scientific Interest. Here, more than 50 pairs of White-headed Ducks nest, with wintering concentrations usually over 100. In 1985, breeding took place in the Marsimas del Guadalquivir, the first recorded nesting in their traditional site for many years.

The White-headed Duck is one bird worth looking for elsewhere in Andalucía, even on isolated or seasonally flooded lagoons. As the population expands, so there is the possibility that new areas will be colonised. Like the Marbled Teal, this is an ICBP Red Data Book bird, so the Spanish population is of increasing international importance.

White-headed Duck

PURPLE GALLINULE
Calamón *Porphyrio porphyrio*

Although common and widely distributed in sub-Saharan Africa,India and the Far East, Australia and New Zealand, this giant rail is only found in Europe in southern Spain, Portugal and Sardinia. Its stronghold is the Marismas del Guadalquivir but it also occurs at a scattering of other sites in Andalucía (particularly in the Guadalquivir valley) where suitable habitat can be found: it likes brackish or freshwater lakes, surrounded by dense stands of reeds. In Spain it is typically shy and wary and reluctant to show itself; it is usually best looked for in the early morning and late evening. This is in contrast to its behaviour elsewhere where it is often bold and easy to see.

Purple Gallinules are largely sedentary, making local movements (often on foot) as marshes dry out in the summer, returning when winter rain brings fresh floods. However, there must be some dispersal as new reservoirs have been colonised in Andalucía and there have been a scattering of records away from the regular breeding areas. In Cataluña, an ambitious re-introduction scheme is attempting to establish this species into the Aiguamolls de l'Emporda, a freshwater marsh which should provide a suitable habitat. This scheme started in 1989 with the first release of 38 birds from the Doñana National Park. All these birds have been ringed. Several similar projects have now been started, and breeding has been confirmed at Albufera de Majorca.

Purple Gallinule

Crested Coot

CRESTED COOT
Focha Cornuda *Fulica cristata*

The inappropriately named Crested Coot is a widespread breeding bird south of the Sahara, with a small remnant population in Morocco, and an even smaller one in southern Spain. One hundred and fifty years ago it was much more common in Spain than it is today, occurring as far north as Valencia. Now, no more than a few pairs of birds remain and the best place to look for them is the Laguna de Medina, near Jerez de la Frontera, where in recent years one or two pairs have nested annually.

However, the Laguna de Medina also supports a population of several hundred common Coots (peaking at up to 25,000), so picking out the Crested Coots can be extremely challenging. Despite its name this species does not have a crest but does sport two red knobs on the crown. These are almost impossible to see at any range during the non-breeding season and are hardly obvious even in the spring. The best field marks are the Crested Coot's more erect neck posture, which makes it look as if it has a slightly longer neck than a common Coot, and its more angular-shaped head.

BAILLON'S CRAKE
Polluela Chica *Porzana pusilla*

Few birds are more difficult to observe than this sparrow-size rail. It is a rare summer visitor to western Europe but little is known of its movements. It is thought to breed at a number of sites in Iberia, although firm evidence is hard to obtain.

CRANE
Grulla Común *Grus grus*

When La Janda, in southern Andalucía, was drained in the early 1950s, the last-known breeding area for Cranes in southern Europe was lost. Although no longer Spanish breeding birds, Cranes are important visitors, with most of the west European population of this species - some 40,000 to 50,000 birds - wintering here. The first of the wintering flocks arrive in mid-October but it is not until the end of November that the majority of the population is present. Some birds continue farther south, for this is a regular migrant across the Strait of Gibraltar.

The main wintering areas are in Extremadura

Baillon's Crake

Cranes

and adjacent areas of Portugal and Andalucía. The migrating birds fly through the Pyrenean passes and there are a number of traditional resting places used each year as the migrants move south. The Embalse de Buendía, for example, a wide reservoir on the River Guadiela in Castilla-La Mancha, is an important resting station for many thousands of cranes. During the last 20 years the northern resting points have become increasingly popular with Cranes as wintering areas, especially in the Gallocanta area of Aragón. This is because Gallocanta (a large brackish lagoon, protected as a national game reserve) provides a secure roost. There is also good foraging on surrounding arable fields where the cranes are unpopular because of the damage they inflict on young cereals.

However, the majority of birds still scatter to individual wintering sites throughout Extremadura where flocks of anything from 500 to several thousand birds may be found. Smaller numbers move south to Andalucía and it is notable that a sizeable flock winters in La Janda.

For the first part of the winter the Cranes feed on stubbles, gathering cereal grains, before moving into the open holm oak forests where they forage for acorns. Early in the New Year they move back to arable land, taking germinating grain and vegetable crops. Northward passage, which starts in late February, is much more contracted than the autumn migration with the great Vs and long, straggling, lines of birds heading back to France, then north to breeding areas in Scandinavia.

GUILLEMOT
Arao Común *Uria aalge*

Guillemots are generally thought of as birds of the northern seas so it comes as a surprise to discover a small population breeding as far south as the Berlengas Islands off the coast of Portugal. The Iberian population is both small and rapidly decreasing; in 1939, there were an estimated 6,000 pairs in the Berlengas Islands, but today that figure is closer to 70. The Spanish population was estimated at over 2,000 pairs 30 years ago, but is now down to around 30 pairs. Sadly, the future for this diminishing species in Iberia is far from bright and extinction before the turn of the century seems likely.

Guillemots are rarely recorded south of the breeding area, although they have been recorded south to the Strait of Gibraltar, and the great majority of auks observed from the coast in the western Mediterranean are Razorbills.

Guillemots

BIRDS OF PREY

HONEY BUZZARD
Halcón Abejero *Pernis apivorus*

Honey Buzzards are among the last of the migrants to return to Europe from their wintering grounds in west and central Africa. The first migrants cross the Strait of Gibraltar in late April, but the peak of the passage takes part in the first 10 days of May, when up to 12,000 birds have been counted. In contrast, the rather more concentrated southern passage, which takes place within the last few days of August and the first 10 days of September, has produced seasonal totals of more than 100,000 birds.

How many of those migrants which cross the Strait remain in Spain is debatable for the majority move on north into Europe, most to France, where this species is a common breeding bird. However, a conservative estimate suggests at least 1,000 breeding birds, concentrated mainly in northern and central Spain. Honey Buzzards are shy woodland birds, favouring mature woods where their main prey - wasps - can be found in abundance. As a result they are generally absent from the more arid areas of the country.

Compared with most raptors, Honey Buzzards are not particularly aerial as they find much of their food on the ground. Their presence is most easily detected when the male performs his distinctive wing-clapping display, flying high above the breeding territory. With practice this is an easy bird to identify, despite its superficial resemblance to the common Buzzard. The small head and slender neck, coupled with the longer tail and wings more pinched at the base, help separate the two species.

BLACK-SHOULDERED KITE
Elanio Azul *Elanus caeruleus*

Thirty years ago it was uncertain as to whether this attractive species was a regular nesting bird in Iberia, but we now know it to be a scarce, localised, but quite widespread breeding bird throughout much of Spain. Although it may have been overlooked in the past, numbers have certainly increased with many records away from former strongholds (principally in Extremadura), and the greatest concentration in the Campo Aranuelo, the wide plain to the south of the River Tiétar. The first recorded European nesting of this species outside

Left: *Honey Buzzard*

Black-shouldered Kite

the Iberian Peninsula was in 1989, when a pair nested in France, and no doubt derived from Spanish stock.

Black-shouldered Kites are characteristic birds of the open plains, preferably with a few scattered trees for nesting cover. In Spain they can often be found hunting over extensive corn fields where their distinctive, rather owl-like, flight action makes them easy to spot even at long range. They spend a great deal of time hovering, often with their feet trailing below.

This is a common bird in much of sub-Saharan Africa, and it also occurs throughout India, south-east Asia and Australia, as well as parts of both North, Central and South America. It is rare in North Africa, with little evidence of much interchange between the Spanish and Moroccan populations. Its rarity in Europe has always been surprising and there seems no reason why the population should not continue to increase and expand in southern Europe as this species can happily live in close proximity to humans.

BLACK KITE
Milano Negro *Milvus migrans*

The Black Kite is one of few European raptors to have increased its numbers and expanded its range in recent years. It is a widespread and common summer visitor to Iberia, with the first birds returning from their wintering grounds in tropical Africa in mid-February. The peak time for passage is March, gradually falling away during April and May. Many of the migrants which cross the Strait of Gibraltar are probably heading north into France; the majority remain in Iberia, where estimates put the population at about 25,000 pairs.

This bird is widespread throughout Iberia but tends to avoid mountainous areas, or the coastal zones, and displays a marked liking for wetlands and waterways. Though a regular passage migrant through the Balearics, it does not nest in the islands.

Unusually for birds of prey, Black Kites are happy living in close proximity to humans and refuse tips are one of their favoured hunting grounds. At migration times it is not unusual to see flocks of as many as 3,000 Black Kites feeding and wheeling over rubbish tips in Andalucía.

Though easy to identify, this species can be mistaken for a dark-phase Booted Eagle, or even a distant Marsh Harrier. The longer, deeper-forked tail of the Red Kite helps separate the two in silhouette: if seen well, the Red Kite is obviously much redder, with distinctive white markings on the underside of the primaries.

Although juvenile Black Kites have been recorded heading south on passage as early as late June, most leave during the first half of August and are soon followed by the adults. The passage, which involves around 60,000 birds, continues into September and October, though with rapidly falling numbers . Occasionally some birds winter in Iberia.

Black Kite

Red Kite

RED KITE
Milano Real *Milvus milvus*

Iberia's Red Kite population is almost certainly the largest in the world, for this handsome bird is restricted almost entirely to Europe with just a small population in North Africa and the Canary Islands. Many authors suggest that numbers in Iberia have declined during this century but thanks to the recent, more enlightened attitude to birds of prey, it seems that the decline has been halted and in certain areas this species is thriving. Young birds taken from Spanish nests are currently being flown to Britain to take part in an ambitious re-introduction scheme.

To see Red Kites in abundance go to the foot-hills of the Pyrenees, especially along the valley of the Rio Aragón around Jaca, where this species is very common. In winter, the valleys of the Ebro and the Duero support high numbers, sometimes as many as 100 birds in 100sq km. Elsewhere, it is most frequently seen in the central, west and south-west, favouring open, lightly-wooded country. Nowhere is it more abundant than on the Balearic island of Menorca, where the nesting density is very high and the birds are not generally disturbed.

Population estimates vary but the actual size is probably around 6,000 pairs - possibly more. Numbers are augmented in winter by migrants from France, Germany and Switzerland, though in recent years increasing numbers of Red Kites are believed to be remaining close to their breeding grounds in northern Europe.

A small number of birds move south into North Africa - it is a scarce but regular migrant across the Strait of Gibraltar, with most of the southerly records in September, and the peak return passage in April.

Lamergeier

LAMMERGEIER

Quebrantahuesos *Gypaetus barbatus*

Spain is the European stronghold for this, the rarest and most spectacular of Europe's vultures. Once widespread throughout the mountainous areas of Spain, numbers had declined sharply even 100 years ago and the decline continued for the first half of this century. Although some of the persecution was deliberate, many birds died from eating carcasses treated with strychnine, aimed at fox or even wolf control. Today, thanks to careful protection, numbers are increasing, and around 55 pairs nest in the Spanish Pyrenees, where this species is easy to see at such sites as Ordesa National Park and at Riglos. Breeding pairs are carefully monitored and many young birds have been marked with conspicuous wing tags as part of a long-term study. Population growth is slow, as only one chick is reared a year and young birds do not nest until they are five years old.

Lammergeiers are sedentary (though they do range over large territories) so there is little prospect of re-colonisation of such former strongholds as the Sierra del Pinar, Sierra Nevada or Sierra de Cazorla without help from humans. It is possible that a few Lammergeiers still survive in the Sierra de Cazorla - a single bird was recorded there on many occasions in the mid-'80s and this was certainly the last known Spanish breeding locality for this species outside the Pyrenees.

EGYPTIAN VULTURE

Alimoche *Neophron percnopterus*

Spain is the European stronghold for this, the smallest of the vultures to occur in Europe. As usual, population estimates vary but most recent counts suggest that 1,000 pairs nest in Spain, with 40-60 pairs in Portugal. However, there has been a noticeable decline in recent years, a reflection of changing agricultural practices as well as improved hygiene. In northern Spain special feeding projects have undoubtedly helped this species, to some extent making up for loss of natural food.

The Egyptian Vulture is adaptable in its choice of habitat, and is found in farmland, open steppe and even mountainous terrain. It usually nests in shaded caves within cliff faces and traditional sites are used year after year. They nest sparsely and in scattered pairs throughout much of Spain, from Andalucía to Cantabria. They also nest on Menorca, with perhaps 20 pairs, where the population is resident; it has been extinct on Majorca for some years. Elsewhere in Iberia the birds are migratory, returning from mid-February onwards, with a peak in March. The southward passage starts in August, with most in September; few birds remain in Spain by mid-October.

GRIFFON VULTURE

Buitre Leonado *Gyps fulvus*

Vultures thrive in backward countries so it is hardly

surprising that numbers of Griffon Vultures have fallen sharply in Iberia since the turn of the century. Today, however, there may be signs that the decrease has slowed down, if not stopped entirely, especially as new, more enlightened attitudes to birds of prey become more widespread. Estimates of Spain's Griffon Vulture population range from 2,000 pairs to a more realistic 5,000 in some 140 colonies; Portugal has an additional 100-150 pairs.

Domestic stock forms the bulk of this species' diet, though in big-game hunting areas Red and Fallow Deer carrion can be important. In the past, many birds were killed by eating poisoned meat, laid out for wolf or fox control, but mortality from such causes has declined . However, improved methods of animal husbandry have resulted in far fewer carcasses available for the vultures to clear away so special vulture feeding projects can be important in maintaining local colonies.

In Iberia, griffons almost always nest on cliff faces, rarely in trees. This restricts their breeding range, but they are wide-ranging birds and will feed up to 100km from their colony. The colonies vary in size: most are around 15 to 20 pairs, some over 100. Birds from different colonies will join together at a carcase and it is still possible in parts of Spain (especially in the Marismas del Guadalquivir) to see gatherings of over 100 birds.

In Spain, this species is most common in Andalucía, Extremadura and the Pyrenees; it is very rare in the north-west and scarce in the north. Its Portuguese stronghold is in the Upper Douro Valley, but birds are regularly seen in the Algarve. Most of the population is resident, though there is some southward movement in the autumn, chiefly by juveniles and immatures, some of which cross to North Africa.

BLACK VULTURE
Buitre Negro *Aegypius monachus*
The largest of Europe's raptors, the Black Vulture is also one of the rarest. With an estimated 365 pairs, the Spanish population is by far the largest in western Europe. Its strongholds are in Castilla-La

Left: *Griffon Vulture*   *Black Vulture*

Mancha (the Sierra del Chorito has at least 70 pairs, the second largest colony in Spain, while there are at least 20 pairs in the Sierra de los Canalizos); Extremadura (Monfragüe is reputed to be the best area in the world for this species, with at least 120 pairs); and Andalucía (especially the Sierra Madrona, the Sierra Morena in Córdoba and the Picos de Aroche), with outlying populations in the Sierra de Guadarrama, of 30 pairs. Although numbers appear to be relatively stable, the current population is very much smaller than at the turn of the century.

A small population survives in the mountains in the north of Majorca, but this is in sharp decline. As recently as 1967 a census revealed 67 birds, but today the figure is 20 birds and just 2 breeding pairs so eventual extinction seems inevitable. Black Vultures occur regularly in Portugal, especially close to the Spanish border (the Sierra de San Pedro, on the Portuguese border, is a stronghold with 60 breeding pairs), but there is no evidence that this species breeds in the country.

Black Vultures are colonial nesters, usually building their bulky nests in the tops of trees, sometimes no more than 5 metres off the ground, but usually rather higher. Cliff nesting is rare in mainland Spain, but occurs regularly on Majorca. Spain's Black Vultures are largely sedentary, adults rarely moving far from their nesting areas; in contrast, immature birds do disperse widely from where they were hatched and most of the birds that winter in the Marismas del Guadalquivir are immatures. This species is slow to mature, not breeding until about six years old so the immature birds have a long period in which to wander.

The main threat to the Black Vulture is from intensive forestry, especially the extensive planting of alien conifers and eucalyptus trees in their breeding areas - some traditional nest sites have been lost due to forestry activities. These birds are also dependent on sufficient supplies of carrion, usually from cattle and deer, so changes in land use and animal husbandry can also be a threat to their long-term survival.

Short-toed Eagle

Marsh Harrier

SHORT-TOED EAGLE
Aguila Culebrera *Circaetus gallicus*

Spain's breeding population of this species (3,000 pairs) is by far the most important in western Europe. A migrant, the first birds start to return from their wintering grounds in the northern tropics of Africa in mid-February, with peak numbers crossing the Strait of Gibraltar in March. Migration continues long into the spring, but these late birds are invariably immatures. Short-toed Eagles are slow to mature, not breeding until three, or possibly four, years of age and some of these birds may remain in Africa during the northern summer.

Short-toed Eagles are widespread breeding birds throughout Spain, though they are scarce or absent from much of Portugal. Their favoured habitat is arid, open country with scattered woodland; hilly, undulating areas are particularly popular, as they produce good thermals for hunting. Reptiles - particularly non-venomous snakes - are the favoured prey. Much of the prey is found on the wing, often by hovering, and the distinctive hovering flight, with legs dangling, often allows this species to be identified at great range.

The nest, usually in the crown of a tree, is often used again and again. Once fledged, the chicks remain with their parents, migrating south with them from late August and into September. Only a few stragglers remain into October, and winter records are unusual. Not only does the French population of some 1,000 pairs migrate through Spain, but birds ringed in Poland have also been recovered in this country.

MARSH HARRIER
Aguilucho Lagunero *Circus aeruginosus*

Drainage of wetlands has led to a major decline in numbers of nesting Marsh Harriers in Iberia and the total population is probably no more than 500 pairs. Wherever marshes or lakes are fringed by reeds, however, this species is certain to occur. Indeed, in some areas, such as the Marismas del Guadalquivir, it can be quite common.

Marsh Harriers are only partially migratory, with some birds remaining on the breeding grounds throughout the year. Many of these wintering birds may be migrants from northern Europe, perhaps replacing the breeding population. There is a marked passage across the Strait of Gibraltar in the autumn, with peak passage in October. The return starts as early as February, the majority of birds moving through in March.

HEN HARRIER
Aguilucho Pálido *Circus cyaneus*

Although often thought to be a bird more typical of northern Europe, this handsome species is a widespread breeding bird in northern Spain where at least 1,000 pairs are thought to nest. In Navarra, for example, it is almost as widespread as the closely related Montagu's Harrier with some overlap of breeding territories. A few breeding pairs can be found in northern Portugal, most notably in the Geres Mountain National Park.

The Hen Harrier is an adaptable species, able to breed wherever there is sufficient open ground for hunting. Extensive cereal-growing areas are favoured and the chief threat to breeding success is when fields are combined before the young harriers have left their nest, which is invariably built on the ground.

The breeding birds disperse throughout Iberia in winter so can be encountered almost anywhere, although marshes and wetlands are favoured hunting areas. Wandering birds from France and northern Europe also winter in Spain, while there is a regular but small passage of birds across the Strait of Gibraltar to North Africa, with peak passage periods in March and October.

Hen Harrier

Montagu's Harrier

MONTAGU'S HARRIER
Aguilucho Cenizo *Circus pygargus*

Although easily confused with the Hen Harrier, this migratory species is a lighter-built, more elegant, bird. Like the Hen Harrier, Montagu's Harrier is a hunter of open country but it is generally found in damper areas than the Hen: broad river valleys and uncultivated plains are favoured, though it will also breed in grasslands and cereal fields. It is widespread in Iberia but is generally absent from the north of the country, where the Hen Harrier takes its place.

The first migrant birds of this species start to return from their wintering grounds in tropical West Africa in March, with peak passage in April. Many of these birds move on through Spain to breeding grounds in northern Europe, including France, Germany and the Netherlands, but around 4,000 pairs nest in Iberia.

Montagu's Harriers are typically birds of the steppe country, most often found in areas with good populations of bustards and sandgrouse. They particularly favour areas where cereal fields are interspersed with areas of uncultivated ground. Their Iberian stronghold is Extremadura: the undulating steppes of Fuente de Cantos, near Montemolín, for example, have around 50 breeding pairs.

Similar population densities can be found at Granja de Torrehermosa, Peraleda de Zaucejo and Zorita, although the best area is almost certainly La Serena, with at least 200 pairs. Changing agriculture and more intensive cereal growing pose a serious threat to the future of this species in Iberia.

GOSHAWK
Azor *Accipiter gentilis*

Despite its size, the Goshawk is one of the easiest raptors to overlook - it is a secretive bird especially when nesting. Estimates put the Iberian population at around 3,000 pairs, but this figure is no more than a rough guideline. However, the Goshawk is certainly a widespread species throughout Iberia, occurring where suitably extensive forested areas exist. It is seldom found far from cover, but will readily hunt fields adjacent to woodland.

While northerly populations of Goshawks are migratory, birds in southern Europe seldom disperse far after nesting. There is a small passage through the Pyrenees and the Strait of Gibraltar, with a few birds crossing to North Africa in September and October, and returning north again in March and April.

Goshawk   Right: *Golden Eagle*

GOLDEN EAGLE
Aguila Real *Aquila chrysaetos*

Spain's population of more than 900 pairs of Golden Eagles is by far the most important in western Europe. In the 1970s this species was thought to be declining for a variety of reasons, including myxomatosis in the rabbit population, direct and indirect persecution from man and habitat change. Twenty years on, the decline certainly seems to have been arrested. Human persecution is no longer such an important factor and, now that predator control by poisoned baits is at last disappearing, numbers may have even slightly increased.

Golden Eagles are widespread throughout Spain and can be found in almost all of the major mountain ranges, from the Picos de Europa in the north to the Sierra Nevada and Serranía de Ronda in the south. Numbers are particularly high in the Pyrenees, where this bird is relatively easy to see. For example, the area of San Mauricio (which includes the National Park of Aigües Tortes) has at least 18 breeding pairs, while the area around Ordesa National Park has at least 5 pairs. In contrast, this is an extremely rare bird in Portugal, with only one or two breeding pairs. It has been extinct in the Balearics for many years.

Although Golden Eagles are typically birds of rugged, mountainous country, they also occur in more low-lying areas if the human population is sufficiently sparse. Most adult eagles remain within their home territory throughout the year, but young birds disperse more widely and wandering immatures may appear considerable distances from known breeding areas. There is little evidence of movement between the North African and Spanish populations.

SPANISH IMPERIAL EAGLE
Aguila Imperial *Aquila adalberti*

Until recently the white-shouldered Spanish Imperial Eagle was thought to be a distinctive race of the widespread Imperial Eagle, *Aquila heliaca*, but it is now generally regarded as a separate Spanish endemic species. As such, it qualifies for entry to the ICBP Red Data List, for the most recent population estimates suggest just over 100 pairs exist in Spain

and possibly another one or two pairs in Portugal. This species formerly bred in north-east Algeria and northern Morocco, but has not done so for many years.

This species' Spanish strongholds are in central Spain - El Escorial is especially important with at least 10 pairs, as is the Sierra de Guadarrama. There are several other sites in Castilla-La Mancha where this species occurs but some of the best areas are in Extremadura. Both Monfragüe and the Sierra de San Pedro have at least 8 pairs. There is also a number of sites in Andalucía, of which the best known is the Coto Doñana which has some 16 pairs. This is certainly the easiest place to find this species and it is a bird that the visitor to the Doñana National Park can be confident of seeing at any time of the year.

Thanks to protection numbers of these fine birds are probably stable, possibly even increasing slightly. For example, in 1883 there were thought to be no more than two breeding pairs in the Coto Doñana owing to intense persecution and for a long time this number varied between two and four. There was a gradual increase in the 1950s which has continued until the present so that Doñana now probably carries as many breeding territories as it can. Twenty years ago most estimates put the total Spanish population at no more than 100 birds. Today's figure is based on more precise census work and may not indicate an increase in numbers.

The main threats to the future of the Spanish Imperial Eagle are changes to its favoured habitat - rolling, lightly wooded countryside. Forestry monocultures do not suit this species. Changing attitudes to birds of prey ensure that more birds survive to adulthood, but as they do not breed until they are four or five years old any increase in numbers is slow. Juvenile birds wander quite widely but the adults usually stay close to their breeding territory throughout the year. There is a scattering of records of this species crossing the Strait of Gibraltar to North Africa, nearly all of which concern immature birds.

Right: *Spanish Imperial Eagle*   Overleaf: *Booted Eagle*

BOOTED EAGLE
Aguila Calzada *Hieraaetus pennatus*
Conflicting estimates put the Iberian population of this buzzard-sized eagle at anything from 5,000 to 9,000 pairs. The latter figure may well be the most likely, for this is a widespread and adaptable species found throughout much of the country. In many parts of Spain it is the most commonly seen large raptor and it is certainly the most numerous of Iberia's five eagle species.

Booted Eagles are summer visitors to Iberia, returning from March, but with peak numbers in early April. As this is a fairly scarce breeding bird in France (around 250 pairs), most of the returning birds head for breeding territories in Spain. The

Bonelli's Eagle

favoured habitat for this species is hilly or mountainous areas, with forest and woodland interspersed with open areas; it dislikes extensive forests, especially of similar-aged trees. Nests are usually built in trees on warm, south-facing slopes. Where the right mixture of habitats is available, it will nest at sea-level, as it does in the Coto Doñana. Southward migration starts in mid-August, peaking in September, but birds can still be seen as late as the beginning of November. The September passage can be concentrated, with as many as 1,000 birds in a day crossing from the Strait of Gibraltar.

This species is particularly common on the Balearic island of Menorca. This population, is unusual in being resident throughout the year. Wintering birds are scarce in mainland Spain.

BONELLI'S EAGLE
Aguila Perdicera *Hieraaetus fasciatus*
Bonelli's Eagle is a widespread species, found from Portugal east to China. It is widely distributed throughout India and in Africa, south of the Sahara, as well as a sizeable population in Morocco. In Europe it is restricted to the Mediterranean zone but is invariably rare and localised. Only in Spain does a healthy population survive, estimated at around 700 pairs. A number of pairs also breed in Portugal.

For many years Bonelli's Eagle has been the most heavily persecuted of all the eagles, as its favoured prey of Red-legged Partridges and rabbits makes its unpopular with hunting interests.

Although low mountains with steep rock faces and deep ravines are the most favoured habitat in Spain, this is an adaptable bird and will readily hunt over open plains and steppe country, ranging up to 25km from its nest site. During the winter Bonelli's Eagles will range even more widely, suggesting that the liking for mountains is mainly a breeding requirement, for cliff ledges are the most favoured nesting site in Spain.

Bonelli's Eagles are widely distributed in Spain but can be elusive and difficult to find. They are easy to identify: the pale body and contrasting underwing pattern of the adult is distinctive as is the powerful flight, which recalls an accipiter or even a falcon rather than an eagle. They are also frequently seen in pairs. Spain's population is resident, the adults usually remaining in the loose vicinity of the nesting territory throughout the year and the young dispersing more widely.

OSPREY
Aguila Pescadora *Pandion haliaetus*
At one time Ospreys nested widely around the coast of Iberia with scattered eyries on the Cantabrian coast, as well as sites such as Cape Trafalgar and Gibraltar, where the last nest was recorded in 1933. Today this spectacular bird no longer breeds in mainland Spain, though two to three pairs still nest on the south-west coast of Portugal. The Spanish stronghold lies in the Balearics, where several pairs are resident, although there has been a recent decline. Ospreys last nested on Formentera in 1968, on Ibiza in 1975.

Many migrant birds pass through Iberia: passage across the Strait of Gibraltar starts in mid-February, peaks in March and continues well into May. A few non-breeding birds may summer on the Mediterranean coast and there are also many records of birds over-wintering, with a few areas (such as Paul de Boquilobo Natural Reserve in Portugal and the Guadiaro Estuary in Cádiz Province, Spain) usually holding at least one wintering bird.

Autumn passage starts in mid-August and peaks in September. Ringing recoveries suggest that most of these migrants are from the Scottish, Norwegian and Swedish populations, heading for wintering grounds in West Africa. As the Scottish population continues to grow, so does the chance that migrant birds will linger longer in Iberia and may eventually start nesting again: there is still plenty of suitable habitat and the more enlightened attitude to birds of prey should ensure that nesting birds are not shot, as they were in the past.

LESSER KESTREL
Cernícalo Primilla *Falco naumanni*
Once an abundant breeding bird throughout much of Iberia, numbers of Lesser Kestrels have fallen sharply in the last 25 years. Though the current

population of around 45,000 pairs is by far the largest in western Europe, it is much reduced - in the early '60s it was estimated at around 100,000 pairs.

The reasons for the decline are clear: increased use of insecticides, both on the breeding grounds in Iberia and the wintering areas of Africa, have not only poisoned the birds, but destroyed much of their prey - for this bird is chiefly an insect feeder and in Spain invertebrates have been found to make up at least 85% of their diet. Grasshoppers and crickets make up the most important prey items.

Lesser Kestrels are partial migrants: most of the young birds and as many as 75% of the adults

Osprey

winter in the savannahs of tropical Africa. This species is an abundant visitor to South Africa, but the birds may well be from the Asiatic or east European populations. Most of the population returns to Iberia in March and remains until September, but many colonies hold birds throughout the year.

Lesser Kestrels are gregarious, usually hunting in loose flocks over open countryside. They invariably nest in colonies, sometimes of scores of pairs, usually on cliff faces or even buildings, for this is a bird that is happy to live alongside humans. Seville Cathedral, for example, has long held a colony.

The Lesser Kestrel's range takes in much of central and southern Iberia; it does not occur in the north and is a rare bird in the north-east, with just a scattering of nesting sites in Navarra.

Lesser Kestrel

KESTREL
Cernícalo Real *Falco tinnunculus*

The shape of the hovering Kestrel is a familiar sight over open countryside and farmland in many parts of the Iberian Peninsula. It is a bird which nests equally well in trees and on cliffs but, unlike the Lesser Kestrel, it is usually solitary. The Iberian Kestrel population is among Europe's largest and numbers are further increased in winter by central and north European birds. In contrast to the Lesser Kestrel, then, the Kestrel is present in all areas throughout the year. Although most visiting birdwatchers are familiar with the Kestrel and seek the exotic Lesser Kestrel, they should keep in mind that both species are present and should always check any kestrel carefully to avoid possible misidentification.

Kestrel

ELEONORA'S FALCON
Halcón de Eleonor *Falco eleonorae*

The Balearics, with some 250 pairs nesting in 24 colonies, are the Iberian stronghold of this highly specialised falcon. Most of these colonies are on the steep cliffs of north-west Majorca, but colonies can also be found on the islands of Vedr and Vedranell, and de Tagomago, off the coast of Ibiza; in the Archipiélago de Cabrera, to the south-east of Majorca; and Dragonera, off Majorca's western tip.

Surprisingly perhaps, this species does not nest on Menorca, where it is a scarce visitor.

The world population of Eleonora's Falcon numbers about 5,000 pairs, the majority found in the eastern Mediterranean. The entire population is thought to winter in Madagascar, while a paucity of records from Africa suggest that the birds migrate at a great height. Most leave Madagascar in March, to return to their breeding cliffs in the Balearics in late April and early May. Breeding is delayed until late summer to enable the young birds to be fed on the abundant supply of migrants, that move south across the Mediterranean. As a result, these falcons remain until late October, and even early November, before leaving for Madagascar. During both spring and autumn migration passage birds may be found on the Spanish Mediterranean coast.

Many of the Balearic colonies are inaccessible, but one of the best sites to watch these aerobatic birds is around the lighthouse at Cabo Formentor on Majorca. They are invariably exciting birds to watch, if not pursuing quarry then chasing each other in fast-flying groups. During the autumn they are most active early in the morning, intercepting small migrants heading for the safety of land. In mid-summer the most important prey are newly-hatched swifts but wheatears, redstarts, yellow wagtails and willow warblers are taken in considerable numbers as the autumn migration gets under way.

PEREGRINE
Halcón Peregrino *Falco peregrinus*
During the '60s and early '70s, when the Peregrine

population of Europe was in sharp decline, Iberia's Peregrines remained largely unaffected by pesticide poisoning. As a result, the population became by far the most important in Europe, with an estimated 2,000 pairs. It is a scarce bird in Portugal but widespread in Spain, breeding almost anywhere suitable nesting sites can be found (usually on cliff faces, rarely in trees). This bird nests early, often with the clutch of three or four eggs completed by the end of February.

Today the population remains largely unchanged - recent estimates are around 1,600 pairs, suggesting a more conservative count rather than a decline in the last 20 years. This population is largely resident, remaining in the vicinity of the breeding area throughout the year. Iberian Peregrines are of the Mediterranean sub-species *brookei*, which is generally smaller than north European birds, and darker both above and below, some with a rufous breast. Wandering peregrines from northern Europe do occur regularly in the country in winter and there have been ringing recoveries of Scandinavian-ringed birds in Spain. A single recovery of a bird ringed in Northern Ireland was found in Portugal.

Eleanora's Falcon

Peregrine

LAND BIRDS

CAPERCAILLIE
Urogallo *Tetrao urogallus*

Spain's small Capercaillie population, restricted to the Pyrenees and the Cantabrian Mountains, is generally regarded as a post-glacial relic, isolated many thousands of years ago. The combined populations are thought to number around 1,000 birds. In Asturias this species is widely distributed, if hard to see. Among the most important areas are the national game reserves of Degana (with around 50 males), Somiedo (about 120 males) and Riaño (some 180 males). Here, the birds are found in typical Cantabrian deciduous woods, of beech, oak, silver birch and holly, generally between 1,200 to 1,600m. This deciduous habitat contrasts with that elsewhere in the Capercaillie's range, where it is almost always found in association with coniferous trees.

In the Pyrenees the Capercaillie is found in more typical pine-forest habitat and at a generally higher altitude than in the Cantabrian Mountains (typically between 1,700 to 2,000m) and though widely distributed, the population is low. The most important area is the San Mauricio-Bohí-Beret area, which includes the National Park of Aigües Tortes, with a minimum of about 200 males.

Changing patterns of land use, tourism and hunting pressure have all contributed to a gradual decline in Capercaillie numbers in the last 30 years, making this one of the most vulnerable, and endangered, of Spanish birds.

RED-LEGGED PARTRIDGE
Perdíz Roja *Alectoris rufa*

In economic terms the Red-legged Partridge is by far the most important of Spanish birds, as well as being one of the most characteristic species of the extensive cereal growing areas of the Meseta. It is a common, highly successful, species, well-adapted to life in this arid area, with hot summers contrasting with cold winters. Where protected, it can become abundant and Spanish partridge shooting has a reputation for offering some of the best -- and most expensive - game shooting in the world, attracting enthusiasts from the rest of Europe as well as the USA.

Many of the partridge shoots take in vast areas of countryside, with scores of beaters being used to drive the birds in the direction of the guns. Bags of several hundred birds in a day are quite usual but it should be noted that many areas are only shot over once in a season, leaving a large stock of birds on the ground. Unfortunately, increasing commercialism of the partridge shooting has seen

Left: *Capercaille*

Red-legged Partridge

hand-reared birds being liberated in an attempt to boost numbers. In addition, there has been a general decline in traditional keepering (which includes supplying water for the birds during the summer and destroying ground predators such as ocellated lizards, which are responsible for destroying many clutches). Disease has been spread to the wild partridges by the released birds, while numbers of released hybrid Red-leg x Chukar partridge (which are easier to breed in captivity than pure Red-legs) are also a threat to the genetic purity of the resident birds.

BARBARY PARTRIDGE
Perdiz Moruna *Alectoris barbara*

It is almost certain that the Barbary Partridges of Gibraltar, the only ones in mainland Europe, were introduced by the British from North Africa in the eighteenth century.

Today, a population of about 60 pairs survives on the less disturbed areas of the Upper Rock, Windmill Hill and the slopes above Catalan Bay. Its preferred habitat is low scrub and rocky slopes, where it is relatively easy to see by the patient observer. In the autumn and winter coveys of up to 25 birds can be found. The urban development of La Linea means that there is little possibility of the partridges spreading north into Spain. Red-legged Partridges do not occur on Gibraltar, so any partridge seen there will be this species.

QUAIL
Codorníz Común *Coturnix coturnix*

Quail breed throughout Iberia, although they are far more often heard than seen. The cock's liquid, constantly repeated "wet-my-lips" call is a familiar

Quail

sound in all the cereal-growing areas, most often heard at dusk. Though fields of cereals are the most favoured habitat, Quail can also be found in clover fields and even meadows where there is sufficient cover.

The migratory movements of Quail remain a mystery. The majority of Iberian birds are summer visitors, returning to their breeding areas in March and moving back south in September. Although these birds are thought to be trans-Saharan migrants, the situation is complicated by the fact that small numbers of Quail regularly winter around the Mediterreanean coast of Spain, while some birds (including young of the year) are believed to move north from Morocco into Iberia (and even farther north) in mid-summer.

ANDALUSIAN HEMIPODE
Torillo *Turnix sylvatica*
Arguably the most elusive and least known of all European breeding birds, the Andalusian Hemipode remains a mystery species. In the 1800s

it is known for certain that it occurred in very small numbers in southern Andalucía and southern Portugal, but recent records are few and far between. In 1875, it was described as locally numerous in south Cádiz, and it is certainly this area, north to Jerez de la Frontera, where it should be looked for. In 1989, several birds were observed in the Coto del Rey, and also in the adjoining Coto Doñana.

The Andalusian Hemipode is a shy, secretive ground bird, difficult to flush because of its marked reluctance to fly. It resembles a small quail and, like that species, it favours low scrub, grass fields and stubble fields. Although believed to be sedentary in Spain, there is little evidence to prove this is the case.

A small population may persist in North Africa, but to be sure of finding this species it is necessary to travel to sub-Saharan Africa or to India, where it is widespread and sometimes quite common. Outside Europe it is generally known as the Little Button Quail.

LITTLE BUSTARD
Sisón *Tetrax tetrax*

Iberia's Little Bustard population almost certainly exceeds 50,000 birds, which makes it of global importance. This handsome bird is typical of rolling, grassy, steppe country readily using extensive cereal fields for both feeding and nesting. Little Bustards favour small hills as observation posts, which can be good places to look for them, especially in the spring when the male performs his simple display. The mating call is a short, dry snort, which can be surprisingly far-carrying - sometimes as far as half a kilometre or more. At the same time the cock inflates his neck, and occasionally jumps into the air with a flash of white wings, though some do far more jumping than others.

Although they are ground-dwelling birds, Little Bustards fly readily and in the spring males frequently indulge in aerial chases. As they fly, so the cock's wings make a creaking sound, created by the fourth primary which is shorter and narrower than the rest. Single birds will often fly considerable distances and in areas with high populations it is quite usual to see birds flying about.

Breeding starts in late March, with the typical clutch of five eggs. Incubation takes 22 days and, as the young are able to leave the nest soon after hatching, Little Bustards usually have mobile young long before the harvesting of cereal fields takes place.

After breeding, flocks will join together, dispersing from breeding territories and concentrating in favoured wintering areas, most notably in Extremadura and Andalucía. Up to 3,000 birds, for example, can be found on plains bordering the River Guadiana close to the Portuguese border. However, by far the most important area for this species in Iberia is La Serena, where as many as 20,000 birds can be found on the undulating, treeless grasslands.

Little Bustard

GREAT BUSTARD
Avutarda *Otis tarda*

Great Bustards were once widespread throughout much of continental Europe but as they have given way to civilization, the great plains of Spain and Portugal represent their last stand. This makes the joint Spanish and Portuguese populations of tremendous international importance: Spain has some 8,000 birds, Portugal close to 1,000.

Great Bustards are typically birds of open, undulating, steppe country, favouring well-drained soils and disliking rocky areas. One of their essential requirements is a broad panoramic view, so they are never found in wooded areas although they will, on occasions, feed in olive groves and cork oak plantations.

In Portugal the main strongholds are in the Alentejo, with the plains of Castro Verde particularly important. In Spain, the greatest numbers are found in Castilla y Léon and Extremadura. Of the former, the most notable areas are Tierra de Campos (with around 2,000 birds) and the extensive, semi-arid plains of Villafafila, (about 1,000). In Extremadura, the undulating plains between Cáceres and Trujillo hold up to 1,000 birds, and similar numbers can be found on the plains between the River Tajo and the Sierra de San Pedro. Any suitable habitat in Extremadura is likely to hold this species, which can also be found in parts of Andalucía (with a tiny remnant population surviving in La Janda), and on the steppes of the Ebro valley, in Navarra and Aragón.

Because of their size and their liking for open countryside Great Bustards are not hard to find in areas where they are numerous but can be very difficult to see in more marginal areas. At long range a flock of feeding bustards can be mistaken for grazing sheep.

Unlike the more northerly populations of Great Bustards, those of Iberia are largely sedentary, dispersing after breeding when they may join into sizeable flocks. This is little evidence to back claims that part of the population moves to North Africa in the winter. The survival of Iberia's bustards depends not simply on species protection, but on preserving their habitat. Intensive cultivation, constant disturbance by grazing animals or farming activities, as well as tree-planting and even the installation of fences, are not tolerated by these shy, wary birds. Although they are now protected from hunting this is not necessarily a good thing: as a game bird, they had considerable commercial value to the landowner but this no longer applies. The long-term future of this magnificent bird remains uncertain, especially as farming in both Portugal and Spain modernizes and intensifies under the encouragement of the E.E.C.

Great Bustard

PIN-TAILED SANDGROUSE
Ganga *Pterocles alchata*
This species no longer breeds in Portugal but is still widespread throughout Spain wherever suitable habitat can be found. Although it prefers more sandy, desert-like, steppes than the Black-bellied Sandgrouse there is a considerable overlap of range with that species and in certain areas the two sandgrouse can be found in close proximity to each other, though generally they are in slightly different habitats.

Pin-tailed Sandgrouse

Like the Black-bellied Sandgrouse, it needs water and will fly considerable distances to favoured drinking places. Most drinking takes place early in the morning so this is a good time to look out for this handsome bird, easily recognised by its long tail streamers and pale belly.

For much of the year Pin-tailed Sandgrouse can be found in large flocks but these decline in size as the days get longer, finally breaking up into pairs from mid-March onwards. After breeding the flocks join up again and there is some dispersal. A number of birds, for example, move to the dried-out Marismas of the Guadalquivir in late summer and early autumn.

BLACK-BELLIED SANDGROUSE
Ortega *Pterocles orientalis*
These birds range from North Africa to central Asia but in western Europe they are found only in Iberia. This species is generally the rarer and more localised of Iberia's two sandgrouse, although in certain areas it is more widely distributed than the Pin-tailed. In Navarra, for example, the atlas of breeding birds records 29% of 10km squares holding Black-bellied Sandgrouse, compared with just 8.5% for the Pin-tailed.

Black-bellied Sandgrouse can be found at higher altitudes than the Pin-tailed and are more tolerant of vegetation cover. Their typical habitat is steppe or semi-desert, even poor grazing land. Because of their cryptic plumage they are difficult birds to spot on the ground, and the best way to find them is to watch for birds flighting to water early in the morning; they are strong flyers and will go as far as 60km to find water.

Their choice of habitat often overlaps with that of Great Bustards, so areas with strong bustard populations in the Alentejo, Extremadura, Castilla y León, Navarra and Aragón are all likely to hold this species. One of the most notable areas is La Serena in Extremadura. In parts of their range Black-bellied Sandgrouse are highly migratory, but Iberian birds remain within their breeding ranges throughout the year. Birds do flock in the winter but they are less gregarious than the Pin-tailed Sandgrouse.

Black-bellied Sandgrouse

Right: *Great Spotted Cuckoo*

GREAT SPOTTED CUCKOO
Críalo *Clamator glandarius*

This species is best regarded as a wet-season migrant to Spain and Portugal, as the adult birds return from their wintering grounds in Africa from November onwards and many will move south again in late June and early July. However, many young birds remain until late autumn, so there may be only a few weeks in early autumn when this species is absent from southern Spain.

Great Spotted Cuckoos parasitise Magpies, Azure-winged Magpies and Carrion Crows, so are most numerous where populations of these three species are highest, such as in the Coto Doñana. They can be found throughout Spain and Portugal except for the far north, although they generally avoid forests or mountainous areas over about 500m. Numbers are highest in the south and west, but in recent years there has been evidence of an increase in the north-east of Spain.

It is an easy bird to locate - not only is it large and conspicuous, but also extremely noisy, the harsh chattering call frequently attracting one's attention.

Eagle Owl

EAGLE OWL
Búho Real *Bubo bubo*

Although persecution has reduced Eagle Owl numbers throughout Europe, the rugged and remote mountains of Spain have long remained a major stronghold for this spectacular species. It remains widely distributed throughout the country, with relatively dense populations in some areas - as many as four pairs in 3sq km in favourable sites in the Sierra Morena and Montes del Toledo. In Portugal it is a rare bird although it may well be under-recorded. It is absent from the Balearics.

The best way to locate Eagle Owls is by sound: the continuous "oohu-oohu-oohu" call is far-carrying and can be heard up to 4km away in favourable conditions. However, despite its size, spotting this bird can be difficult as it is a nocturnal species and in Iberia usually hunts under cover of darkness. Roosting birds generally hide away in crevices on cliff faces but some will sometimes perch more prominently on a pinnacle or lookout.

Spain's Eagle Owl population is probably somewhere between 500 and 1,000 pairs: after a long period of decline due to persecution it is probably now stable. In some areas of Spain the young are still taken from their nests and kept by gamekeepers as decoys, luring magpies and crows to their deaths.

LITTLE OWL
Mochuelo Común *Athene noctua*

Unlike other small European owls, this bird does not require trees for either nesting or roosting. As a result, it is the most widespread owl in Iberia, commonly found even in arid, treeless areas but absent from forested mountain zones. In some areas this bird can be quite abundant and, because it is only partially nocturnal, it is the most commonly seen owl. Instead of hiding away by day, many birds roost in relatively conspicuous places, such as on the tops of disused farm buildings or hay ricks. They are fierce, opportunistic, feeders quite prepared to tackle prey almost as large as themselves; recorded prey ranges from young rabbits to birds up to the size of thrushes. In Spain, research has shown that invertebrates make up 94.7% of their diet by number, but only 33.6% by weight.

With their short, rounded wings and dipping flight, Little Owls are not suited to long-distance migration, so Iberian birds are resident, with only small local movements. This inability to cross open stretches of water explains their absence from the Balearics and other offshore islands.

Little Owl

Red-necked Nightjar

SCOPS OWL
Autillo *Otus scops*

There is no more characteristic sound of warm Mediterranean nights than the musical, yet monotonous, piping of Scops Owls. This is a widespread, often very common, species throughout much of Iberia. It favours cultivated areas, citrus groves, plantations, and even gardens and city squares. In some areas, such as the foothills of the Pyrenees and Cantabrian Mountains, as well as in Andalucía, it is particularly abundant.

Scops Owls are strictly nocturnal and, because they merge so well with their background, very difficult to find roosting during the day. They start calling as dusk starts to fall and can be lured into view by imitating their simple call.

In the northern half of Iberia this species is a summer visitor, although some birds remain in the Algarve, southern Spain and the Balearics throughout the year.

RED-NECKED NIGHTJAR
Chotacabras Pardo *Caprimulgus ruficollis*

This species is an Iberian speciality - except for a few pairs on the French Mediterranean coast, it nests nowhere else in Europe. A summer visitor, it returns in April and May to its favoured nesting areas, which range from olive groves and cork oak scrub to stone pine woods and even semi-desert areas. It prefers drier, more sunny areas than the common Nightjar, which also occurs widely in Iberia. Red-necked Nightjars remain on the breeding grounds until September, when southerly passage starts, continuing on until November.

A larger bird than the Nightjar, it is more sandy coloured and has a rusty neck and parts of the head. However, the best way to tell the two species apart is by voice: the Red-necked Nightjar's song is a distinctive and continuous "kutuk-kutuk", which sounds rather like a double blow against a hollow tree.

Red-necked Nightjars are found throughout much of Iberia but are more numerous in the south than the north, where they are largely replaced by Nightjars.

PALLID SWIFT
Vencejo Pálido *Apus pallidus*

Along much of the Mediterranean and south Atlantic coast of Iberia, and in the Balearic Islands, Pallid Swifts outnumber, and often replace, the common Swift. Unlike the latter, Pallid Swifts return from their (largely unknown) African wintering grounds as early as February and remain until late autumn, with some birds often lingering until early November or even later. They are double-brooded, with the young of the first brood fledging in July and those of the second in October. In contrast, common Swifts return to Iberia in April, are single brooded and most of the breeding birds have gone south again by mid-July.

Although Pallid Swifts closely resemble common Swifts in both appearance and habits, with practice they can best be told apart by their rather slower flight action, slightly broader build, paler plumage and different voice. The familiar scream is deeper, less shrill, then the Swift.

ALPINE SWIFT
Vencejo Real *Apus melba*

This, the largest of the European nesting swifts, is a widespread breeding bird in much of Spain and also occurs at a number of sites in Portugal. As the name suggests, Alpine Swifts favour mountainous areas, but they will also nest on sea cliffs and even in buildings. The latter habit is relatively new and has allowed these birds to colonise lowland areas from which they had been absent.

Iberian birds start to return to their nesting areas in early March; although the autumn migration may start in late July, it does not peak until September. Alpine Swifts are highly specialised feeders, often foraging considerable distances from their colony, which makes it difficult to estimate population numbers.

Pallid Swift

Alpine Swift   *Right: Bee-eater*

WHITE-RUMPED SWIFT
Vencejo Cafre *Apus caffer*
When this species was first found nesting in southern Spain in 1964, it was misidentified as the Little Swift, which also has a white rump. This is an understandable mistake as Little Swifts nest commonly in North Africa, right up to the Strait of Gibraltar. In contrast, White-rumped Swifts are rare birds in Morocco, where they were recorded nesting for the first time only in 1979.

It is now known that a small population of White-rumped Swifts nest in southern Spain. The first nests were found in Cádiz Province, but small populations have been found more recently in the provinces of Córdoba and Almería. Almost all nests have been in those of Red-rumped Swallows, and the breeding season is delayed until after the swallows have finished nesting. As a result, White-rumped Swifts do not generally start to return to their Spanish nesting sites until late May, remaining until late summer. Numbers of White-rumped Swifts appear to be increasing One of the most reliable areas to look for this species is around the town of Zahara, to the south of Cádiz; another is the woodland around Castellar, also in Cádiz Province.

BEE-EATER
Abejaruco *Merops apiaster*
The first Bee-eaters start to return from their wintering grounds in tropical Africa in mid-March, but most of the birds do not appear until April. Thanks to the combination of brilliant plumage, distinctive voice and conspicuous habits these birds are not easily overlooked. They nest throughout much of Spain, Portugal and the Balearics, avoiding only the north and the higher mountain ranges - they like sheltered, sunny areas and avoid exposed or cool places, therefore they seldom breed at any altitude. Bee-eaters are quite catholic in their choice of habitat; their preferred terrain is a mixture of cultivation and woods but they can also be found in open steppe country and even in clearings in pine and oak forests.

These birds are colonial nesters, excavating their nest burrows in sand pits or river banks, but sometimes in almost level ground. They generally remain within 1km of their nesting colony, seldom ranging more than 4km away.

Autumn passage starts in late August, peaks in mid-September and is almost completed by October. Bee-eaters usually migrate by day at a considerable height, and it is not unusual to hear migrating birds calling high overhead, but to be unable to see the birds themselves.

ROLLER
Carraca *Coracias garrulus*
Although widespread throughout much of Iberia (except the north and west), the Roller is a scarce breeding species and not particularly common in any one area. They favour warm, summer climates, so tend to be found away from oceanic influences and from high mountains. The most favoured habitats in Spain are stone pine woodland and areas with scattered cork oak; elsewhere grazed pastures and cultivated river valleys are also favoured. Rollers avoid grassy steppes because these areas lack suitable nesting trees (they nest in holes) and look-out posts to hunt from.

Rollers are summer visitors to Iberia, the first birds not returning to their breeding areas until late April and early May. This is the best time to see the

spectacular aerial display which gives the bird its name. The noisy, rolling displays are most often provoked when an intruding bird enters an established territory.

By late July the first Rollers are already moving south, and almost all have gone by the end of August. It was once thought that Iberian birds migrated diagonally across the Sahara to winter in East Africa, but it is now believed that this population winters in West Africa.

HOOPOE
Abubilla *Upupa epops*

No bird is more characteristic of the Mediterranean than the Hoopoe where it is a common and conspicuous bird. On hot summer days its far-carrying "hoo-hoo-hoo" call frequently reveals its presence. Hoopoes are widespread throughout Iberia, and only in the north are they less numerous and rather localized. Their favoured habitat includes open, cultivated, land and plantations such as olive groves and vineyards but they are quick to take advantage of golf courses, for example, feeding on the watered greens and fairways.

Iberia's Hoopoes are partially migratory. A significant proportion of the population moves to Africa to winter south of the Sahara, although many birds remain in the southern half of the country throughout the year. Some birds may well be migrants from France and west-central Europe, replacing the breeding birds during the winter. In the Balearics, for example, Hoopoes decline in numbers during August but pick up again in November, suggesting that the breeding birds have been replaced by migrants or that they have moved away to avoid the summer drought.

Northward migration is most apparent during February and March and continues through until early May. In the autumn, August sees peak movement but migration continues until October.

Left: *Roller*   *Hoopoe*

WRYNECK
Torcecuello *Jynx torquilla*

If it were not for the male Wryneck's persistent and loud spring song, this is a bird that could easily be overlooked. Although it has declined in numbers in recent years, the Wryneck remains a common breeding bird throughout much of northern Spain (it was found in more than 80% of squares in Navarra, for example) and in parts of Portugal (particularly the Algarve). Wrynecks also breed occasionally in the Balearics and in southern Spain, where they are common migrants on autumn passage as they are throughout much of coastal Spain.

Many of these autumn migrants will be birds from west and north-west Europe, which generally migrate to Africa through Iberia. Autumn passage can be protracted, with the earliest migrants being young birds from first broods which have dispersed soon after fledging. The majority of birds move south in October. While most Wrynecks winter in Africa, small numbers remain in southern Spain throughout the winter. Spring migration starts as early as February but peak numbers cross the Strait of Gibraltar in March.

BLACK WOODPECKER
Pito Negro *Dryocopus martius*

Spain has three isolated populations of Black Woodpeckers: in the Cantabrians, the Pyrenees and the Sierra de Guadarrama. Although there are a number of records from north-west Portugal there is no proof of this species having nested in the country. Nowhere is this species common, for territories are large, but Black Woodpeckers invariably reveal

Left: *Wryneck*   *Black Woodpecker*

their presence with their loud, far-carrying calls and their powerful drumming. They are sedentary birds, remaining within their breeding territories throughout the year. However, the young birds will disperse quite considerable distances away from where they were hatched.

Black Woodpeckers require mature climax forest, of mixed beech and fir trees, but in the Cantabrians they can be found in pure stands of beech. In the Pyrenees they occur right up to the tree line, but they can also be found at low altitudes in many of the Pyrenean foothills where suitable forests exist.

MIDDLE-SPOTTED WOODPECKER
Pico Mediano *Dendrocopos medius*
These birds are found on the extreme western edge of their range in Spain. A small population still survives in the foothills of the Pyrenees but here they are extremely rare. Only in the beechwoods of the Cantabrian mountains is this species reasonably common and relatively easy to find. There is also a small, isolated, population in the oakwoods of the Montes de Toledo.

Middle-spotted Woodpeckers are small and easily overlooked, frequently feeding in the leaf canopy rather than on the main trunk of the tree. The male's spring territorial call frequently reveals his presence; being rather slow and nasal, it is quite unlike that of any other European woodpecker. When seen well, the Middle-spotted Woodpecker is a noticeably smaller, more compact, bird than the Great Spotted (which also occurs in the same habitat), with a noticeable rosy flush to the underside, the latter a feature seldom shown in field guides.

WHITE-BACKED WOODPECKER
Pico Dorsiblanco *Dendrocopos leucotos*
This is the largest of the spotted woodpeckers found in Europe; it is also the rarest. The Iberian population is small and restricted to the Pyrenees, where it occurs from 800 to 1,600m. White-backed Woodpeckers have specialist habitat requirements, favouring old, untouched stands of pure beech, sometimes mixed with silver fir. They require a high proportion of dead or diseased timber within their range, so are absent from managed forestry plantations.

White-backed Woodpeckers are sedentary, remaining within their breeding territory throughout the year. They are best looked for on south-facing slopes where in spring the males can be located by their drumming, which is both slower and longer than that of the Great Spotted, accelerating towards the end. The total Spanish population is unlikely to be more than 100 pairs.

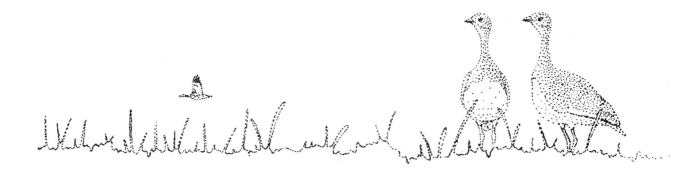

Waders, Gulls and Terns

BLACK-WINGED STILT
Cigüeñuela *Himantopus himantopus*

No bird is more characteristic of the coastal salt pans than this handsome species but Black-winged Stilts also breed at many inland sites both in Spain and Portugal. The Spanish strongholds are the Ebro Delta and the Marismas del Guadalquivir, both of which hold at least 1,000 pairs, though estimates of the total Iberian population vary from 12,000 to more than 20,000. The first figure has been confirmed by a recent survey (1989). Numbers have increased, and new areas colonised, in the past 20 years.

These birds are opportunists readily colonising recently flooded land where conditions are suitable, but disappearing again once the area dries out. After nesting, much of the Iberian population moves to Andalucía to moult, with the adults arriving in late July and the young birds of the year following on later. Most of these birds will move farther south once they have moulted but small numbers can usually be found in southern Spain and Portugal throughout the year. Most of the migrants return as early as March.

AVOCET
Avoceta *Recurvirostra avosetta*

Although often found in company with Black-winged Stilts, Avocets have more specialised requirements, preferring barer, more open areas, with only the sparsest vegetation - a liking they share with flamingoes. Thus these birds are generally outnumbered in Iberia by the more adaptable, opportunist stilt, but numbers of breeding birds are relatively high. Both the Ebro Delta and the

Left: *Black-winged Stilt*   *Avocet*

Marismas del Guadalquivir hold around 400 breeding pairs, while the numerous salt pans of the Bahía de Cádiz hold many hundreds of pairs. Smaller colonies can be found elsewhere though the majority are close to the coast.

After they have finished nesting (in late July) there is a general southerly dispersal and concentrations of birds will occur in rich feeding areas. Numbers of birds in Iberia are increased by migrants from northern Europe, and there have been Iberian ringing recoveries of Avocets from Britain and even Austria.

The majority of these birds will move on to wintering areas in Senegal but significant numbers winter on the estuaries of southern Portugal: the Tejo estuary regularly holds 9,000 birds but peak numbers can be twice as high. The Sado estuary, to the south, has a wintering flock of around 1,200 birds, rising to 2,200.

STONE CURLEW
Alcaraván *Burhinus oedicnemus*

Iberia is the west European stronghold of this strange, crepuscular wader. Its retiring behaviour, coupled with its superbly cryptic plumage, make this a difficult species to count or even estimate numbers but it is a widely distributed bird throughout much of Spain and Portugal. Stone Curlews are noisy at night and it is this wild, far-carrying, calling that often reveals their presence.

So long as the terrain is dry and open the Stone Curlew is relatively adaptable in its choice of habitat and can be found in extensive cereal fields, grazed pastures, along dried-up river beds, or in

Stone Curlew

poor stony pastures and in rolling steppe country. Numbers are probably highest in Extremadura and Andalucía, although small, but important, breeding populations can be found in the Balearics, on both Menorca and Majorca.

Most of the Iberian population is probably resident and winter flocks can be found in many favoured areas. Ringing has shown that more northern populations migrate through Iberia in October and November en route to wintering grounds in Africa while some remain for the winter, as British marked birds have been recovered in Spain in December and January. The majority of the small British population may winter in Iberia as these birds are usually back on their breeding grounds in late March, when most of the birds that have wintered in Africa are only just moving north.

COLLARED PRATINCOLE
Canastera *Glareola pratincola*
This attractive species is on the north-western edge of its range in Iberia. Specialised habitat

requirements limit this bird's range; it favours flat, extensive areas, preferably with shallow water, but will also occur on dried-out flood plains. It also likes a warm, Mediterranean, climate so is absent from many areas which might otherwise appear to be suitable.

In Iberia, Pratincoles are most numerous in the Marismas del Guadalquivir, where several hundred pairs nest, although smaller scattered colonies can be found throughout Andalucía north to Extremadura and at a few sites in the Algarve. The most northerly breeding population is on the Ebro Delta, where there are two colonies, the most important of which is threatened by holiday-home developments. The total Iberian population fluctuates but is probably around 2,000 pairs.

Pratincoles are gregarious birds and the most aerial of the waders, catching much of their prey (small insects) on the wing. They are early migrants, breeding soon after they return from their African wintering grounds in order to make the most of remaining winter floods. As soon as they have finished breeding they move to a moulting area, most typically on a salt pan or fallow field, before moving down river valleys towards the coast. The Albufera de Valencia is a well known collecting area for post-breeding birds. Most have left Iberia for Africa by mid-September.

Collared Pratincole

KENTISH PLOVER
Chorlitejo Patinegro *Charadrius alexandrinus*
Although this is one of the most widely distributed of waders, found in both North and South America, northern Africa as well as in many parts of Asia as far east as Japan, the west European population is small - probably numbering fewer than 3,000 pairs. The majority of these nest around the coasts of Spain and Portugal though there are several inland colonies in Spain, particularly where the salinity of the water is high and keeps the waterside vegetation in check.

Kentish Plovers favour smooth, sandy beaches for nesting but on the Spanish Mediterranean coast are most frequently found on salt pans, where they are less often disturbed. Possibly the most important Spanish nesting area is the extensive salt pans of the Bahía de Cádiz which has several hundred nesting pairs. Many move south into Africa after nesting but important numbers winter in Andalucía and on the estuaries of Portugal.

LITTLE RINGED PLOVER
Chorlitejo Chico *Charadrius dubius*
These birds nest along the river valleys of most of the major rivers of Spain and Portugal and can frequently be found nesting on patches of gravel or shingle exposed by the falling river. They also nest along the Mediterranean coastline: rarely on the beach itself but usually in association with coastal pools or lagoons. Although Little Ringed Plovers are often found in company with Kentish Plovers, the latter favours more saline areas, the former freshwater.

Little Ringed Plovers are mainly summer visitors to Iberia, leaving the breeding areas soon after nesting. A few remain in Andalucía all winter. Autumn passage begins in mid-July and by August

Kentish Plover at nest

Little Ringed Plover at nest

most are on the move. At this time peak numbers are found in the Balearics: these birds have probably bred in France or Britain and are migrating to Africa on a south-easterly route. There is little evidence that birds from northern Europe migrate through mainland Spain. They return from Africa early in the year, with many birds back on their breeding territories in early March.

SLENDER-BILLED GULL
Gaviota Picofina *Larus genei*
This species has a fragmented distribution in Europe, breeding in a few widely scattered localities around the Mediterranean. Thus, the Spanish population of a mere 450 pairs may be small but is one of the largest and most important in western Europe. Most of these birds nest in the Ebro Delta, where the population has grown from 12 pairs in 1975 (the first year breeding was recorded) to 429 pairs in 1988. The best places to look for this elegant bird are the Sant Antoni salt pans, on the Trabucador spit and at the Punta de la Banya.

A few pairs still nest regularly in the Marismas del Guadalquivir. Until recently, this bird was regarded as a summer visitor though the wintering grounds remained a mystery. However, an increasing number of birds are seen in the vicinity of the Ebro Delta throughout the winter.

Slender-billed Gulls

AUDOUIN'S GULL
Gaviota de Audouin *Larus audouinii*

Just 20 years ago this species was regarded as one of the world's rarest birds, with an estimated population of 1,000 pairs all nesting within the Mediterranean. Today, we know that the total population is certainly well over 12,000 pairs and may be as high as 20,000, reflecting not only more comprehensive census work and the increased skills of observers in recognising this species but also a genuine increase in the population.

At least 30% of the population nests in Spain. Until recently, the Islas Chafarinas, off the north African Spanish enclave of Melilla, boasted the largest breeding colony in the world (2,800 pairs in 1987) but this has been overtaken by the Ebro Delta. Here the first birds nested in 1981, with the initial colony numbering 36 pairs. The following year there were 200 pairs; 546 in 1983, 1,200 in 1985 and 6,714 in 1992. Such a rate of increase is quite extraordinary and not easily explained.

In contrast, the numbers of breeding pairs in the Balearics has remained static. Here there are several sites, the most important of which are on the Archipélago de Cabrera to the south-east of Majorca, with 100 pairs and on the Islas de los Freus (between Ibiza and Formentera) with 135 pairs.

Audouin's Gulls are summer visitors to the nesting areas, arriving in March and early April and leaving soon after breeding is completed in August. They are regular and fairly numerous migrants through the Strait of Gibraltar (where they are present all year) in late summer and autumn, heading for wintering grounds on the Atlantic coast of Morocco, from Cape Spartel southwards.

Audouin's Gull

MEDITERRANEAN GULL
Gaviota Cabecinegra *Larus melanocephalus*
Despite its rather misleading name, this gull rarely breeds in Spain (several records in the Ebro Delta) but is a regular and abundant winter visitor to the entire Mediterranean coast of Spain and the Atlantic coast of Portugal and Spain. However, by far the most important wintering area is between Castellón and Barcelona, with 50,000 gulls making this the Mediterranean's greatest winter concentration.

Most birds spotted off the Iberian coast almost certainly originate from the large Black Sea colonies. One of the most interesting Spanish recoveries was of a bird ringed in the Black Sea as a chick in 1975, caught and released in the Netherlands the following September and found dead near Cádiz two months later.

There is a marked westward passage through the Strait of Gibraltar from late June until mid-August while small numbers are regular through the Strait in the autumn, with a peak in November. The return passage into the Mediterranean starts in February and continues into April.

This species is extending its range in western Europe, so may well become more firmly established as a breeding bird in Spain in future years.

Mediterranean Gull

YELLOW-LEGGED GULL
Gaviota Patiamarilla *Larus cachinnans*
Once regarded as a race of the Herring Gull, this bird is now generally classified as a full species within the complex Herring Gull group. Yellow-legged Gulls nest along much of the northern coast of Spain, at a scattering of sites along the Portuguese coast and at an increasing number of sites along the Spanish Mediterranean coast. The Mediterranean population is of the race *L.c.michahellis*. Colonies also exist on most of the offshore islands; the one on the Islas Chafarinas is particularly large and still expanding, to the detriment of the smaller Audouin's Gulls also nesting on this island group.

Yellow-legged Gulls are sleeker, less bulky birds than the typical Herring Gull of northern Europe and are usually darker on the back. The characteristic yellow legs are not acquired until the bird is a full adult, three years after hatching. However, recent studies have shown that between 5-10% of the Yellow-legged Gulls breeding in Galicia have wholly or partly flesh-coloured legs.

Yellow-legged Gull

GULL-BILLED TERN
Pagaza Piconegra *Gelochelidon nilotica*
Spain's Gull-billed Tern population numbers between 800 and 1,000 pairs, making it the largest in western Europe. However, numbers of this species fluctuate widely, even from year to year. For example, in the mid-'70s as many as 3,500 birds were present in the Lagunas de Fuente de Piedra colony in Andalucía but in recent years the numbers have been very much smaller and in some years none have nested at all. Today this species' stronghold is the Marismas del Guadalquivir, with around 500 pairs nesting, while the Ebro Delta colony numbers around 100 pairs, up from 24 pairs in 1979.

Although generally found near water, Gull-billed Terns frequently feed over land and are often found far inland. Spanish-bred birds are thought to winter in West Africa, while birds from the Danish population certainly migrate through Iberia in both spring and autumn, as has been confirmed by a number of ringing recoveries. Post-breeding dispersion starts as early as late June and by mid-July peak passage is under way. At this time Gull-billed Terns can be encountered almost anywhere as they migrate on a broad front.

LESSER CRESTED TERN
Charrán Bengalés *Sterna bengalensis*
Although generally thought of as a rare vagrant to Europe, this species has nested successfully in Spain,

Gull-billed Tern

Lesser Crested Tern

on the Ebro Delta, in 1979 and 1985 (two pairs) while another pair held territory in 1981. The nearest regular breeding colony to Spain is in Libya and birds from this population pass through the Strait of Gibraltar in May-June and again in August-October, though records from the Iberian mainland are few.

ROYAL TERN
Charrán Real *Sterna maxima*
Until recently this species was regarded as an extremely rare vagrant to southern Spain but observations now suggest that Royal Terns are regular visitors to the Strait of Gibraltar, where they can be locally common between late July and October. These birds are thought to be wanderers from the West African population that breeds on the Banc d'Arguin in Mauretania. Although there are more records on the Moroccan side of the Strait, there have been a number of Spanish sightings from as far north as Huelva and east to the Alborán Sea. It seems likely that this bird will be increasingly commonly recorded now that observers are specially lookout out for it.

Royal Tern

CASPIAN TERN
Pagaza Piquirroja *Sterna caspia*

These birds are scarce passage migrants on both the Atlantic and Mediterranean coasts of Iberia, though this species has exceptionally attempted to nest in the Ebro Delta. The only regular breeding colonies in western Europe are in the Baltic and most of these birds are thought to migrate overland south through central Europe. However, a small percentage of these terns apparently follow the coastline of the North Sea and Atlantic coast, which are the birds recorded in Iberia.   Caspian Terns may be found regularly in winter along the south Atlantic coast, between the Strait of Gibraltar and Portugal.

WHISKERED TERN
Fumarel Cariblanco *Chlidonias hybridus*

This attractive marsh tern is most numerous in India, South and East Africa and Australia but is scarce and localised in Europe. The Spanish population has been variously estimated at anything from 3,600 to 100,000 pairs - the more conservative figure is likely to be closer to the truth.

Caspian Tern

Whiskered Tern

The Whiskered Tern is a bird of open marshland and eutrophic lakes, feeding by hawking insects in the air or snatching prey from the water surface. It breeds at a number of sites in Spain where the conditions are right but the Marismas of the Guadalquivir hold the largest breeding population of several hundred pairs.

These terns are migrants, most returning to their nesting areas in late April. However, a few birds regularly over-winter in southern Spain. Many migrants move on north through Spain to breed in France and this species is notably more common on spring than autumn migration. Autumn passage starts in late July and continues through to October.

SONGBIRDS

DUPONT'S LARK
Alondra Ricotí *Chersophilus duponti*

Shy and elusive, the Dupont's Lark is possibly the most overlooked of all Spanish breeding birds. Several current European field guides totally ignore this species and one states that "in recent years a tiny population has nested in central Spain (only a few pairs)". In fact, a census in the spring of 1988 gave a figure of between 7,000 and 8,000 pairs. However, it is an extremely difficult bird to observe, with disturbed birds running away from the intruder to disappear in cover. Peak activity is at dawn and dusk: during the breeding season song can be heard as early as 04.30 and again at 22.30, although some will sing throughout the day. The song is unlike that of any other European lark and sounds rather more thrush-like, with short trills.

Dupont's Lark is a bird of dry, open, steppe country and typical habitat includes clumps of vegetation, such as *Salicornia* and feather grass, interspersed with open areas. Outside the breeding season this species will flock with Calandra and Skylarks on arable land.

It is worth looking for this lark in any suitable steppe habitat, but its strongholds are in Castilla y León and Aragón, in the upper reaches of the Ebro valley. Its most important breeding area is probably the high limestone plateau of the Altos de Barahona, in southern Soria, with an estimated population of between 2,000 and 3,000 pairs. Other notable areas include the Parameras de Maranchon - Layna, Paramera de Embid, Valeria, Carboneras de Guadazaon and Moya, all in Castilla-La Mancha, and in Aragón, El Saso, Los Monegros, Ballobar, and Belchite - Mediana.

Ambitious EC-funded irrigation projects, allowing cereal growing in the bird's favoured steppe habitat, have already led to a reduction of numbers of Dupont's Lark in Aragón and other populations are equally vulnerable to so-called agricultural improvement schemes. Dupont's Lark was recorded nesting in Portugal in the 19th century, but there have been no recent records.

CALANDRA LARK
Calandria Común *Melanocorypha calandra*
Although a typical steppe species, this lark favours the more fertile grasslands rather than the semi-desert areas and, as a result, can often be found in arable fields. It is widespread over much of Spain and parts of Portugal, generally in low-lying areas below 600m, and it can be quite local and absent from apparently suitable habitat. There has been a noticeable decline in recent years, almost certainly connected with modern agricultural practices.

Difficult to spot on the ground, the Calandra Lark is most easily found in the spring, when the male performs his distinctive song flight. The wings are held rigidly, giving the impression of a much larger bird, while the contrast of the black underwing with the pale belly is quite distinctive.

Calandras are thought to be non-migratory, but after the breeding season they flock together, often mixing with other larks or even Corn Buntings, and may move away from breeding sites. Some of these flocks can be very large, sometimes numbering hundreds of birds.

Calandra Lark at nest

Short-toed Lark

SHORT-TOED LARK
Terrera Común *Calandrella brachydactyla*
Though generally a bird of dry, steppe, grasslands the Short-toed Lark is an adaptable species and in Spain and Portugal often found on arable land - neglected farmland is particularly popular. It is a common and widespread species and in many areas of Spain, the Balearics and Portugal, the most abundant species of lark. It occurs widely throughout both countries though it is absent from the North Atlantic coast of Spain.

Short-toed Larks are migrants with birds returning to their breeding areas in late March and early April. Once breeding has finished in July they join together in flocks, with autumn passage getting underway from mid August and peaking in September. Migrating birds generally fly at low levels and their distinctive finch-like flight call frequently helps identification. They winter to the south of the Sahara.

Lesser Short-toed Lark

LESSER SHORT-TOED LARK
Terrera Marismeña *Calandrella rufescens*
Much more specialised habitat requirements ensure that this species has a more restricted Iberian
range than the Short-toed Lark with which, however, breeding territories frequently overlap. Lesser
Short-toed Larks are birds of treeless steppes but
they prefer barer, poorer and more arid ground
than the Short-toed, also showing a marked liking
for dried-out marismas and saline areas. Where
the two species occur together they do not
appear to compete with each other as they
both feed in slightly different areas.

Unlike the Short-toed Lark, the Lesser is usually regarded as non-migratory, though there may
be some passage of birds to and from North Africa
in spring and autumn.

CRESTED LARK
Cogujada Común *Galerida cristata*
This is one of the most widespread and familiar of
Iberian birds, though confusion with the very similar Thekla Lark often distorts the picture, especially as the two species frequently occur in close
proximity. Crested Larks are generally birds of
open country but also show a liking for areas
modified by human activities, ranging from super-
market car parks to railway tracks. They favour
warm, dusty, places with only sparse vegetation
and are absent from mountainous and wooded
areas.

Iberian Crested Larks are largely resident, the
adults seldom moving far from their breeding areas. Unlike all the other Iberian larks, except Thekla,
this species does not flock. There is some evidence

of autumn dispersal, and even a small passage of birds across the Strait of Gibraltar in spring and autumn.

THEKLA LARK
Cogujada Montesina *Galerida theklae*
Theklas are an Iberian speciality because they do not occur anywhere else in Europe, apart from a tiny population in southern France. This species favours a more varied habitat than the Crested Lark and is generally found in more rocky and bushy terrain, ranging from olive groves to abandoned farmland. Unlike Crested Larks, which like flat ground, Theklas prefer more hilly terrain, often at a higher altitude. There is some overlap of habitat between the two species but it seems unlikely that the two compete with each other. In the Balearics there are no Crested Larks, and the Thekla is very common.

There is some evidence that these birds living at higher altitudes move to lower levels during the winter but otherwise this is a sedentary species, remaining in the same area throughout the year. Some authorities have argued, however, that more Theklas than Crested Larks cross the Strait of Gibraltar in the autumn.

Crested Lark

Left: *Thekla Lark*

Crag Martin

CRAG MARTIN
Avión Roquero *Ptyonoprogne rupestris*

This chunky, dull-coloured, martin is a widespread breeding bird in suitable habitat in both Spain and Portugal. As the name suggests, Crag Martins favour craggy landscapes ranging from sea cliffs to the mountains of the Pyrenees and the Asturias. They prefer sunny sheltered, south-facing, areas and avoid deep shadow or places exposed to strong winds.

Though Crag Martins are the only hirundines to remain in Europe throughout the year, they are partly migratory. Many birds move to lower altitudes during the winter, for they dislike snow, while others migrate south. There is a long-standing winter roost on Gibraltar, attracting up to 3,000 birds at peak periods in December and January. Ringing has shown that this roost includes birds from many parts of Spain, the Balearics, and even France and Italy. These birds feed in Spain during the day and return to the Rock to roost at night. Many Iberian birds undoubtedly winter in North Africa, returning to their breeding areas in February and March.

RED-RUMPED SWALLOW
Golondrina Daurica *Hirundo daurica*

During the present century this species has been extending its range northwards in both Spain and Portugal. Once numerous only in the extreme south, it first nested in Ciudad Real in 1952, central Spain 1951-3 and Girona in 1960. Today, it can be found along the entire Mediterranean coast. It is widespread inland but breeding sites are scattered in the north, and it is much more common in the south. It is an easy species to spot as its flight is distinctively different from that of the swallow, for it appears much slower with frequent long glides.

Red-rumped Swallows are much less dependent on humans for their breeding sites than common Swallows and, though they regularly nest under bridges and culverts, they also use caverns and cracks and fissures in rock faces to build their distinctive nest. This resembles the nest of the House Martin but with a funnel entrance.

Summer visitors to Iberia, the first birds return in mid-February but the peak passage is in April. They remain in the breeding areas until well into September, even early October.

TAWNY PIPIT
Bisbita Campestre *Anthus campestris*

This large, pale, pipit is a widespread breeding bird throughout much of Spain and the Balearics but is rather more localised in Portugal. It is a bird of the

Red-rumped Swallow

grassy steppes, avoiding arid, rocky or mountainous habitat, and most abundant in dry areas with scant vegetation. It is, however, quite adaptable, and can be found in coastal sand dunes, vineyards, cleared woodland, or even by the side of the road.

Its favoured habitat is often shared with such species as Hoopoes, Short-toed Larks and Black-eared Wheatears. This is an easy bird to locate in the spring because the male's distinctive territorial song flight is frequently repeated and accompanied by the slowly repeated song.

Tawny Pipits are generally solitary birds though after breeding they are sometimes found in small, loose, flocks. Iberian birds are migratory, with autumn passage starting in August and continuing through to mid-October. The wintering grounds are thought to be in the Sahel zone of West Africa. The first of the spring migrants do not usually appear before April, many not returning until early May.

Tawny Pipit

SPANISH YELLOW WAGTAIL
Lavandera Boyera *Motacilla flava iberiae*
With its distinctive grey head, white eye stripe and black cheek patch, the Spanish race of the Yellow Wagtail is easily recognised. Although widely distributed in Iberia, many areas are too arid or mountainous for this bird which is reflected in its patchy distribution. Its favoured breeding habitat is damp meadowland, preferably close to shallow water, but on migration it can also be found in dry pastures, often feeding in association with cattle or other livestock.

It is absent from most of north-west and central southern Spain, while in Portugal it is rather localised; it is a common breeding bird in the Balearics.

Several other races of Yellow Wagtail migrate through Iberia, of which the most numerous is the blue-headed (*f.flava*). The range of the Spanish Yellow Wagtail, *iberiae*, also includes southern France and north-west Africa. Passage starts in March, continues through to early June. Autumn migration starts in late August and continues through to mid-October. Most Spanish Yellow Wagtails are believed to winter in West Africa but some may remain in Morocco.

Spanish Yellow Wagtail

Alpine Accentor

ALPINE ACCENTOR
Acentor Alpino *Prunella collaris*
As their name suggests Alpine Accentors are mountain birds, breeding in Spain in mountains generally from 2000m up to the snow line. This restricts the breeding population to the highest ranges: the Pyrenees, the Cantabrian Mountains, the Sierra Nevada and the Sierra de Gredos. Here they can be common but elusive - it is not unusual to hear the birds' rolling, three-syllable, call but to be unable to spot the bird itself. Once found, Alpine Accentors are usually tame and approachable, and easy to identify, though it should be remembered that the closely related Dunnock frequently occurs in the same areas.

After breeding, Alpine Accentors move to lower altitudes and are then more widespread in Spain, though rare in Portugal. They are quite common winter visitors to the Balearics, though most easily found at higher altitudes. On Menorca, for example, the most reliable site to find accentors in winter is on the top of El Torro, the island's highest point. A few winter annually on Gibraltar, frequenting the cliffs, and it seems likely that similar wintering populations can be found around the Spanish coast where suitable habitat exists.

Rufous Bush Robin

RUFOUS BUSH ROBIN
Alzacola *Cercotrichas galactotes*

These birds are among the last of the summer migrants to return to their breeding areas in southern Spain and south-east Portugal, seldom appearing before the end of April or even early May. They are unusual birds in that they show a marked liking for man-made habitats, such as olive groves and gardens, which are often the best places to look for them. Although these birds frequent thick cover they are not shy and the attractive, thrush-like song is usually delivered from the top of a tree or bush, or in the distinctive song flight when the cock glides on raised wings and with fanned tail.

They are localised and seldom common in Spain and are restricted in their range by habitat requirements. Though associated with steppe landscapes these birds like plenty of bushes and trees, or even thickets of prickly pear, and avoid bare plains and mountainous terrain.

Autumn migration starts in mid-August, and continues through to mid-October. The race that breeds in Iberia, *galactotes*, is thought to winter in north-central Africa.

NIGHTINGALE
Ruiseñor Común *Luscinia megarhynchos*

There is no more delightful sound of spring in Iberia than a melody of Nightingales, singing together in competition. Despite their name they sing by both day and night and, the more birds there are, the more they sing. Nightingales are abundant breeding birds throughout Iberia and the Balearics, absent only from the north Atlantic coast. Though they like damp areas, with tangled vegetation by the sides of streams, they can also be found on dry, sunny, hillsides as long as sufficient cover is available. In northern Europe Nightingales are generally regarded as shy, retiring birds, but in Iberia they are often surprisingly bold, singing from exposed perches or even telegraph wires. It is notable that their song period is much longer in southern than in northern Europe, possibly because many birds produce two broods and the cocks thus hold territory much longer.

Although the first birds are back on their breeding grounds in late March, the majority do not return until April. Autumn passage starts in August and continues through to September, but October birds are scarce. Most Iberian birds probably winter in West Africa.

Nightingale at nest

BLUETHROAT
Pechiazul *Luscinia svecica*

Bluethroats are predominantly Asian birds, breeding on a broad band from Scandinavia and Poland east through Siberia to western Alaska; Spain's small population is the most southerly in Europe, as well as the most westerly. These are skulking birds, seldom flying and spending nearly all of their time on the ground. They require dense cover for nesting, and are most easily found when the colourful and unmistakeable cock is singing from his exposed songpost. Their stronghold in Spain is the Sierra de Gredos where they nest as high as 2,000m, generally on dry, stony slopes densely covered in Spanish broom. There is a second, smaller, breeding population in the Cantabrian mountains. Spanish birds are of the white-spotted race (*cyanecula*) which also breeds in central Europe.

Though the majority of European Bluethroats are thought to winter in Africa, a significant number remain in Iberia (mainly southern Spain, the Balearics and western Portugal). Here they are best looked for in damp or marshy areas, again with a profusion of cover. Return passage of migrants extends from late March through to early May; autumn passage is most marked in October.

Bluethroat

Black Redstart

BLACK REDSTART
Colirrojo Tizón *Phoenicurus ochruros*

One of the most familiar town birds throughout Iberia, the Black Redstart is widespread in a variety of habitats, ranging from towns and villages to rocky gorges high in the Pyrenees. In the south they breed only in the mountains. Their most important requirements are commanding song posts, open areas for feeding and plenty of possible nest sites - they frequently nest in walls or roofs of buildings. Often the cock's presence is revealed by his scratchy warble.

Iberia's Black Redstarts are thought to be mainly sedentary, though birds breeding at high altitudes move to lower valleys during the winter. However, there is some movement of birds to and from North Africa, with peak passage in March and mid-October, so some of the population is certainly migratory.

There are two races: the central and south Iberian race, (*aterrimus*), and the northern *gibraltariensis*, which is the typical European race. The former is coal black with a grey crown and contrasting white wing panel, while the latter is not so dark, with off-white wing panels, which are less obvious. Both races have the same bright chestnut rump and tail. Many *gibraltariensis* birds from central Europe winter in southern Iberia.

STONECHAT

Tarabilla Común *Saxicola torquata*

One of the most common of Iberian passerines, the Stonechat's success is due to its adaptability. It occurs in a wide variety of open habitats, from sea level to sunny, south-facing mountain slopes where its requirements of open ground for foraging and plenty of low perches for hunting, can be found.

Iberian Stonechats are mainly sedentary, though there is a marked movement towards the coast in winter. Two races breed in Iberia: on the west coast *hibernans* occur and elsewhere *rubicola* is to be found. The former is the darkest of all the many races of Stonechat, with the least contrast between upper and lower parts. Numbers are augmented in winter by central European birds.

BLACK-EARED WHEATEAR

Collalba Rubia *Oenanthe hispanica*

Considering the abundance of typical wheatear habitat and the number of species in North Africa, it is a little surprising that Iberia has only three breeding species. Of these, the Black-eared Wheatear is the more common and most widespread, occurring everywhere except in areas influenced by the Atlantic. Black-eared Wheatears favour rocky, open, ground and are particularly common on limestone hills and maquis-covered hillsides.

However, they can also be found in lightly wooded country or even steep cliff faces; they like plenty of perches for vantage points and often sit on the top of shrubs or bushes. At higher altitudes

Left: *Stonechat*

Black-eared Wheatear

the Common Wheatear replaces the Black-eared.

These birds are summer visitors, the first migrants returning in mid-March but most appearing in April. Autumn passage starts in August and by September they can be difficult to find in the breeding areas.

The race found in Iberia is *hispanica* but it should be noted that the plumage is highly variable, depending on age and sex, while the males are dimorphic with either a black or pale throat.

BLACK WHEATEAR
Collalba Negra *Oenanthe leucura*
This species is an Iberian speciality for, apart from a few pairs in France, it is found nowhere else in Europe. It is widespread but localised in suitable habitat throughout much of central, eastern and southern Spain but is rare in central Portugal and absent from areas with an Atlantic maritime influence. Its habitat requirements are more specialised than the Black-eared Wheatear's, as it favours arid areas with poor soils, always close to steep rock faces or cliffs.

Iberian birds are sedentary although birds nesting at higher altitudes, such as in the Sierra Nevada, move lower in the winter. Black Wheatears also occur in North Africa but there is no evidence of any interchange between the two populations.

Left: *Black Wheatear*   *Rock Thrush*

ROCK THRUSH
Roquero Rojo *Monticola saxatilis*

These birds breed in all major mountain ranges of Iberia, chiefly from about 1,250m to 2,300m. They favour barren, south-facing, slopes with plenty of screes and boulders but using trees, pylons or telegraph wires as song posts. In suitable areas they can be quite numerous, their attractive song a familiar sound in the mountains in spring.

The first birds return from their wintering grounds in tropical Africa in April and most are back in their breeding territories by the second week of May. They are shy and difficult to approach on the nesting grounds, behaviour which contrasts with their tameness in Africa. Autumn passage starts in August and most have departed by the end of September.

BLUE ROCK THRUSH
Roquero Solitario *Monticola solitarius*

This thrush favours similar habitats to the Rock Thrush, but almost always at lower altitudes and the ranges of the two species seldom overlap. They are found throughout much of Spain though absent from most of the north-west; in Portugal they are rather more localized while they are fairly common in the Balearics. The Blue Rock Thrush favours three principal habitats - sea cliffs, mountain valleys and large (often ruined) buildings thus, infrequently occuring in towns. They are always shy, wary birds, disappearing out of sight as soon as they are aware of being watched. They are relatively easy to find, often perching for long periods on prominent look-out posts.

Unlike the Rock Thrush they are only partly

Blue Rock Thrush

Ring Ouzel

migratory. There is some dispersal from high ground while some birds move south to winter in North Africa. In winter they are more likely to be found away from their typical, rocky, habitat, sometimes occurring in olive groves, for example.

RING OUZEL
Mirlo Capiblanco *Turdus torquatus*
In Spain the Ring Ouzel is restricted as a breeding bird to the Pyrenees and the Cantabrian Mountains, where it is relatively scarce and localized and generally found above the tree line. These birds are partial migrants, most Spanish nesting birds move

to North Africa in the winter though some may remain in southern Spain. Here they are joined by migrants from northern, central and western Europe, many of which over-winter in the mountains of southern Spain.

Ring Ouzels are early migrants, with spring passage concentrated in March and early April when birds returning to north European nesting grounds may be encountered almost anywhere, sometimes in small flocks. These migrants may linger for a few days before moving north. Autumn passage takes place from September through to November.

Cetti's Warbler at nest

CETTI'S WARBLER
Ruiseñor Bastardo *Cettia cetti*

Cetti's Warblers sing throughout the year and it is usually the sudden and explosive burst of song delivered from thick cover which reveals their presence. Found throughout Iberia, they favour thick tangled undergrowth along watercourses or at the side of marshes, but will also occur in gardens where the vegetation is sufficiently lush. They are absent from high ground and arid areas but are quick to colonise a suitable new habitat.

Nervous, secretive, birds, they are often difficult to spot and the observer seldom gains more than a glimpse as the bird dashes from one patch of cover to the next. When seen well, they look rather like small Nightingales, but with broad, rounded, tails. They are often found in the same habitat as Nightingales.

Though resident in Iberia, there is probably some passage to and from North Africa but the bird's secretive behaviour ensures that possible migrants are usually overlooked.

FAN-TAILED WARBLER
Buitrón *Cisticola juncidis*

This tiny bird is the only European species of a principally African group of skulking, grassland, birds. It is widespread throughout much of Iberia, absent only from the north and north-west. Fan-tailed Warblers are birds of open grassland or low-growing crops such as clover and oil-seed rape.

Here they would be easy to overlook if it were not for their distinctive and noisy display. The call note is a hard "tzitt" (hence their alterative name of 'Zitting Cisticola'), usually delivered in a high, jerking song flight.

Although generally regarded as non-migratory, part of the southern Spanish population certainly moves south to North Africa in July and August, presumably to avoid the harsh, arid, conditions of mid-summer. The return movement starts as early as February and takes place by day, with flocks visibly crossing the Strait of Gibraltar in calm weather conditions.

Fan-tailed Warbler

SAVI'S WARBLER
Buscarla Unicolor *Locustella luscinioides*

In parts of central and southern Spain and Portugal, Savi's is one of the most common of reed bed warblers, its distinctive reeling song revealing its presence. Though Savi's Warblers sing by day they sing more continuously at night so nocturnal visits to reed beds will usually give a better idea of how many territorial males there are. The song can be confused with that of the Grasshopper Warbler though it is faster and lower-pitched. The breeding range of the two species does not overlap in Iberia, as Grasshopper Warblers are restricted to the north.

Savi's Warblers winter in tropical West Africa but their skulking habits ensure that they are rarely recorded on passage. Iberian birds are usually back on their breeding grounds in March, returning south in September.

MOUSTACHED WARBLER
Carricerín Real *Acrocephalus melanopogon*

This skulking, secretive, warbler which breeds from the Guadalquivir eastward in a narrow band following the Mediterranean coast, also occurs in the Balearics. Majorca's Albufera has one of the largest known populations in Europe. Being so shy, it is easily overlooked but it is certainly worth looking for in any suitable reed bed habitat within this area. The very similar Sedge Warbler is the species most likely to be confused with the Moustached Warbler, although it does not breed in Iberia but is a passage migrant. The Moustached Warbler's habit of cocking its tail when feeding or excited is a good field mark.

Most Moustached Warblers appear to be resident but there is some evidence of passage in April and from September to early November.

GREAT REED WARBLER
Carricero Tordal *Acrocephalus arundinaceus*

Most warblers are shy and difficult to observe, but not the Great Reed Warbler. Not only is it large but its song is quite extraordinarily noisy while the singing bird invariably perches on a prominent

Great Reed Warbler

Olivaceous Warbler

reed. It is a bird of *Phragmites*, and is quick to colonise new reed beds growing up by the side of reservoirs or lagoons. Its readiness to colonise new habitat ensures that it occurs throughout Iberia where suitable breeding sites can be found.

Great Reed Warblers are summer visitors, arriving from late March through to early May. Return passage starts in August and continues through September. Like other swamp warblers they are capable of long-distance flight so migrants are rarely seen away from their typical habitat. They winter in tropical West Africa.

OLIVACEOUS WARBLER
Zarcero Pálido *Hippolais pallida*
In Europe, Olivaceous Warblers are restricted to

the Balkans and southern and eastern Spain - while common in the east of Spain they are comparatively rare and localized. They are best looked for in olive groves, parks, gardens and scrubby (often damp) woodland, where the rather monotonous, Reed Warbler-like song reveals their presence.

Though the first birds may appear in southern Spain on passage in March, they are generally late migrants, with the main population not returning until early May. Passage has been recorded in Gibraltar until early June, suggesting these are non-breeding birds. The return to the wintering grounds in tropical West Africa starts as early as mid-July, peaks in August and by early September few birds remain. The Iberian breeding birds are of the *opaca* race.

Melodious Warblers at nest

MELODIOUS WARBLER
Zarcero Común *Hippolais polyglotta*

Melodious Warblers show a liking for similar habitat to Olivaceous Warblers but are much more common and widespread, occurring throughout the Iberian Peninsula. They also breed throughout much of France and this population almost certainly moves through Iberia when on migration. Like the Olivaceous Warbler this is a late migrant and though the first birds may appear in early April, peak passage does not take place until early May. The return starts as early as July and continues through to October.

MARMORA'S WARBLER
Curruca Sarda *Sylvia sarda*

Restricted almost entirely to coastal maquis this unobtrusive bird nests in scattered pockets along Spain's Mediterranean coast and in the Balearics. A considerable percentage of the world population lives in Spain, for elsewhere it is only found in Corsica, Sardinia, Sicily, Elba and Tunisia and possibly a few sites on the north-west Italian coastline. It is a bird that is easily overlooked and is never easy to observe. Shy and furtive, it usually keeps out of sight, perching briefly in the tops of pine or juniper trees before plunging back into cover.

Marmora's Warblers are sedentary, and there are few records of these birds wandering away from the breeding areas.

DARTFORD WARBLER
Curruca Rabilarga *Sylvia undata*

Similar in shape and behaviour to Marmora's Warbler, this bird is far more widely distributed throughout Iberia, occurring wherever its favoured habitat of low maquis, or heathy open land, can be found. It is a winter visitor to Majorca, but nests on Menorca. The Dartford Warbler likes arid hillsides, avoiding lush or damp vegetation and can be quite common where conditions suit it. Like Marmora's Warbler, it can be a difficult bird to see; the secret is to remain still and let the bird show itself rather than to try and flush it.

There are two races in Iberia - the brown-backed Atlantic *dartfordiensis* along coastal areas of Portugal, southwestern Spain and the Balearics; and *undata* which occurs elsewhere.

Although juveniles may disperse in the autumn, this a sedentary species, and remains in the same territory throughout the year. There is a regular passage across the Strait of Gibraltar, though this varies in scale from year to year.

Dartford Warbler

Spectacled Warbler

SPECTACLED WARBLER
Curruca Tomillera *Sylvia conspicillata*

Spectacled Warblers are rather localized throughout their Iberian range which extends from southern Portugal, through much of south-eastern Spain and north along the length of the Mediterranean coast. They require dry, even arid, areas with plenty of low, scrubby, undergrowth and spend a great deal of time feeding on the ground or in the lower layers of scrub. They are not usually difficult to see as they regularly perch on the tops of bushes before disappearing to forage below. The song is also delivered from an open perch or during a song flight.

Much is still to be learnt about the movements of this species. Part of the population is thought to remain on the breeding grounds throughout the year, the remainder migrates to Africa. Its main wintering areas are still uncertain; it has been suggested that most winter in the northern parts of the Sahara. However, autumn passage of birds through the Strait of Gibraltar starts in August and continues into October without the well-defined peak typical of trans-Saharan migrants. The birds involved are from the north of the nesting range, in Cataluña or southern France and these may well winter on the southernmost limits of the area.

SUBALPINE WARBLER
Curruca Carrasqueña *Sylvia cantillans*

This attractive species is well-named as it breeds widely in Spain and Portugal, avoiding lowland areas and occuring as high as 1,500m. It favours maquis and dry, sparse, woodland but also occurs in glades within relatively dense pine woods. Usually furtive and difficult to see, the easiest time to find these birds is when the cocks are singing, which can be done either from the tops of bushes or trees, or in short song flights. Females are always difficult to observe and both sexes become shy and elusive after breeding is finished.

These warblers are thought to winter in the Sahel zone of West Africa. They are scarce on southward migration, suggesting that many fly directly to their wintering areas but this species is

Subalpine Warbler at nest

much more common in the spring. Passage starts in March, when most of the males move north to establish their territories before the arrival of the females, which takes place in April and early May.

SARDINIAN WARBLER
Curruca Cabecinegra *Sylvia melanocephala*
Although this species is known to winter in tropical West Africa in small numbers, most birds are resident and remain close to their territories throughout the year. They are by far the most common of the *Sylvia* warblers in Iberia and the Balearics, although they are absent from the north and most abundant close to the Mediterranean. It skulks in dense scrub, bushes and maquis. It is usually shy and difficult to see, most often observed flitting, with half-fanned tail, from one patch of cover to the next. They can be conspicious in the breeding season when males sing from open perches and perform noisy display flights.

ORPHEAN WARBLER
Curruca Mirlona *Sylvia hortensis*

This large member of the *Sylvia* group is a fairly common summer visitor to much of Iberia, except the north, and can be found in higher maquis, open woodland and even olive and cork-oak groves. In spring, the cock's simple but attractive song frequently draws the observer's attention but no bird is better at slipping out of the back of the tree, unseen, than the Orphean - it is a frustratingly shy bird. Interestingly, birds from eastern Europe, *crassirostris*, have a much fuller, more attractive song than *hortensis* which nests in Iberia and south-west Europe.

Spring passage starts in April and continues through to early June. These birds are seldom recorded on autumn migration, suggesting they fly south to their wintering areas in the arid zone south of the Sahara in a single flight.

BONELLI'S WARBLER
Mosquitero Papialbo *Phylloscopus bonelli*

Bonelli's Warbler takes its name from Franco Andrea Bonelli, an Italian ornithologist born in Piedmont in 1784. It is a common bird of mountainous oak woodland throughout much of Iberia, but is unobtrusive and easily overlooked although its song is distinctive.

Spring passage starts late, peaks in April and continues through until early May. The more southerly populations move south first, for by mid-August breeding sites in Andalucía have usually been vacated. By late September most have left for their wintering areas in tropical West Africa.

Left: *Sardinian Warbler*   *Orphean Warbler*

Bonelli's Warbler

Right: Firecrest

FIRECREST
Reyezuelo Listado *Regulus ignicapillus*
This bird's small size means it is easily overlooked, but it is common and widespread throughout much of Iberia where suitable habitat exists.

Firecrests favour forests of evergreen oaks and tree heaths (*Erica arborea*) but they can also be found in coniferous forests where they may overlap with the closely related Goldcrest.

The migratory movements of Firecrests are confusing: many birds can be found in the breeding areas during the winter, though they generally leave the higher-altitude sites. There is a small southerly passage of birds over the Strait of Gibraltar from late September to November, with the return taking place from February to April.

Crested Tit

CRESTED TIT
Herrerillo Capuchino *Parus cristatus*
This bird's rolling call is usually the first sign of its presence, as it is generally unobtrusive and easily overlooked. This is the most specialised of all the European tits, favouring tall, coniferous forest, preferably with a rich mixture of pines and spruces. It occurs in mountain beech woods, but remains close to conifers. In Iberia it also occurs frequently in broadleaved woodland, even in greater numbers than in some pine woods. This is a resident bird, seldom moving from its nesting area.

SHORT-TOED TREECREEPER
Agateador Común *Certhia brachydactyla*
The Treecreeper of northern Europe occurs only in the Pyrenees, its place elsewhere in Iberia taken by the very similar Short-toed Treecreeper. In central Europe this species is usually associated with deciduous woodland, but in the Mediterranean area it readily occupies lowland stone pine forests and even maritime pine woods. Though the Short-toed Treecreeper is never abundant, it is a widespread bird that can invariably be found in all suitable habitat throughout the country.

This species is generally resident but there is some movement south to Africa. It is most easily found in spring when the male's penetrating song advertises his presence.

Short-toed Treecreeper

Wall Creeper

Right: *Penduline Tit*

WALL CREEPER
Treparriscos *Tichodroma muraria*
Instantly recognisable but extraordinarily elusive, this is one of the most sought-after birds of the mountains of northern Spain. It occurs in both the Pyrenees and the Cantabrians, usually breeding above the tree line. The same nesting sites - usually steep cliffs and rocky, shaded ravines - will generally be used in successive years.

In the autumn Wall Creepers move to lower altitudes and can even be found on buildings. Los Mallos de Riglos, in Aragón, is one of the best-known wintering sites, where birds are present from November through to early April. Other traditional wintering sites include cliffs at Montrebei, Siurana and Ports de Beseit in Cataluña.

Some wintering birds disperse distantly from their breeding areas and this species has been recorded regularly in the Balearics. Although Wall Creepers were found breeding in the Sierra Nevada during the last century, none are thought to be breeding there today.

PENDULINE TIT
Pájaro Moscón *Remiz pendulinus*
During the last 30 years these birds have extended their breeding range in Europe and it also seems likely that numbers of nesting pairs have increased in Iberia during this period, though this is one bird which may have been overlooked, and thus under-recorded, in the past.

From April through to late July Penduline Tits are best looked for in poplars growing by the side of river banks, where their attractive pouch-shaped nest, suspended from the outmost end of a branch and generally hanging over water, often reveals their presence. They can be found in suitable habitat along many Iberian rivers, particularly in the catchment areas of the Ebro, Tajo, Guadiana and Duero.

After breeding, Penduline Tits favour reed-beds fringing freshwater lagoons. Many birds move south, and pairs and even small flocks can be found in many Andalusian reed-beds throughout the winter.

GOLDEN ORIOLE
Oropéndola *Oriolus oriolus*

Far more often heard than seen, the Golden Oriole is a common summer visitor to much of Iberia. Absent from upland and mountainous areas, it is generally confined to wooded lowlands and river valleys. This species is a relatively late migrant and the male's beautiful flute-like call is rarely heard before the second half of April. Autumn passage starts as early as mid-August and most have moved south to Africa by early September. It seems likely that the majority of European birds migrate to the east, thus not passing through Iberia, and it is rare to see migrant birds in Iberia once the residents have left.

Despite the male's vivid plumage, this can be an extraordinarily difficult bird to see, for orioles invariably remain out of sight high in the tree canopy. They are most active, and most noisy, shortly after dawn and this is the best time to observe them.

GREAT GREY SHRIKE
Alcaudón Real *Lanius excubitor*

Although generally regarded as a northern bird, this species is widespread throughout much of Iberia and is a familiar sight perched conspicuously on roadside wires. Iberian breeding birds are of the race *meridionalis*. They are darker on the upper parts than northern and central European races and have less white on the shoulders and supercilium. The underside is also a distinctive grey-pink.

Great Greys are birds of open country, but are extremely adaptable and can be found from almost desert-like steppe to lush river valleys. Iberian birds are partial migrants; many move south in the winter, some remain in Spain and others move across to North Africa.

Some birds from central Europe also winter in Iberia. This species does not nest in the Balearics, where it is a passage visitor, occasionally over-wintering.

Left: *Golden Oriole*

Great Grey Shrike

LESSER GREY SHRIKE
Alcaudón Chico *Lanius minor*

This predominantly eastern bird reaches the western edge of its range in Spain, with just three known breeding sites, two of which are in Cataluña. The latter are on the Lleida Plains and at Empordá, where the favoured habitat is olive and almond groves, and mixed pastures. Numbers vary greatly from year to year; they do not arrive until early May and remain until late August or early September.

Identification can be tricky, as the Iberian race of the Great Grey Shrike is quite similar to the Lesser Grey. The best field mark is the Lesser Grey's black forehead, but it also has a noticeably shorter tail and proportionally longer wings than the Great Grey.

Lesser Grey Shrikes have a migration pattern that takes them eastward, across central and southern Europe, so migrant birds are rarely seen west or south of the breeding areas.

WOODCHAT SHRIKE
Alcaudón Común *Lanius senator*

Woodchats are abundant summer visitors to Iberia and are the only species of shrike to breed in the Balearics. Adaptable in their habitat, they frequent open woodland and maquis, but can also be found in cultivated land and even gardens. Unlike the Red-backed Shrike they are birds of the lowlands and are seldom found in mountainous areas. Conspicuous, easily seen and readily identified, this is one bird which is seldom overlooked.

Iberian woodchats winter in tropical West Africa; the first migrants appear in mid-March, with a peak during the second half of April, and passage continues until early June. The return starts late July, most birds moving south during August.

Lesser Grey Shrike

Right: *Woodchat Shrike*

RED-BACKED SHRIKE
Alcaudón Dorsirrojo *Lanius collurio*

These are relatively common breeding birds in the Pyrenees and foothills, west into the Cantabrian mountains, but do not occur any farther south in Spain. As with the Lesser Grey Shrikes, they migrate through Europe and are therefore exceedingly rare in Spain away from their breeding area. They are late migrants, returning to their nesting territories in mid-May and leaving again at the end of August.

Although this species has declined sharply in north-west Europe (it is now lost as a breeding bird in England), the Spanish population remains healthy.

AZURE-WINGED MAGPIE
Rabilargo *Cyanopica cyana*

This species has the most extraordinary range of any bird, for although its range in Europe is restricted to central and southern Iberia the same species also occurs in China and Japan. No-one has ever satisfactorily explained such a highly disjunct distribution. It is possible that this handsome bird was first introduced to Iberia many centuries ago when early explorers were first making contact with the Far East.

Azure-winged Magpies are highly gregarious, social birds which move through the countryside in loose, noisy, flocks each bird gliding from tree to tree in follow-my-leader formation. They favour

Red-backed Shrike

Azure-winged Magpie

areas of continuous woodland, and are rarely found far from trees. Although their preference is for pine woodland, they are quite adaptable and may even be found roving through eucalyptus plantations - one of the few species of bird to use this alien habitat. In Extremadura they are most frequent in oak woods. Flocks vary in size from a dozen birds to perhaps 60 or 70 individuals.

Azure-winged Magpies are most numerous in Andalucía and Extremadura, where they are a frequent host for the Great Spotted Cuckoo. They are absent from high mountains.

ALPINE CHOUGH
Chova Piquigualda *Pyrrhocorax graculus*
One of the most familiar sounds of the high Pyrenees and the Cantabrians is the rolling, piercing, call of the Alpine Chough. Except during the breeding season they are always seen in flocks, usually high above the tree line. They are acrobatic birds, soaring among the mountain tops, playing on the currents of air or suddenly plunging groundwards on closed wings.

Alpine Choughs are sedentary, rarely, if ever, being found away from the mountains. In winter

Alpine Chough

Right: *Chough*

they will move to lower altitudes and will readily forage for scraps left by humans around ski-resorts. Studies have shown that although they have adapted and benefitted from this new source of food, numbers have remained static as this additional food merely complements their natural diet.

CHOUGH
Chova Piquirroja *Pyrrhocorax pyrrhocorax*
Iberia's Chough population is by far the largest and most important in Europe. Typically a bird of rocky gorges, cliffs and rugged mountainous areas, it is also closely associated with the close-cropped grasslands of animal pastures. It is found throughout Iberia where conditions are suitable but is vulnerable to changes in land use and particularly a swing

away from traditional pastoral practices. Choughs depend on close-cropped grassland on which to forage and they thrive on grasslands which are seasonally grazed by mixed flocks or herds of sheep, cattle and horses. As soon as the grazing stops, the pastures no longer provide suitable habitat for the choughs. Thus, the Chough's future in Iberia may well depend on financial support from the EC which ensures the continuance of low-intensity farming.

In the high mountains Choughs frequently associate with Alpine Choughs; with practice, the two can be separated in flight by the latter's longer and more rounded tail. Though the Alpine Chough has a higher, more ringing, call telling the two species apart by voice alone is difficult.

Raven

RAVEN
Cuervo *Corvus corax*
Ravens are the most common of the corvids in many parts of Iberia, suggesting that this might well have been the case elsewhere in Europe before persecution reduced their numbers. However, even here numbers have been reduced during the present century. Much of Iberia provides perfect habitat for this species, with rugged cliffs and mountains for nesting and extensive grazing areas where animal carrion provides a reliable source of food throughout the year. Ravens are adaptable and will readily raid rubbish tips.

The Raven is the only breeding corvid in the Balearics and it is not unusual to see gatherings of 100 or more birds.

SPOTLESS STARLING
Estornino Negro *Sturnus unicolor*
This bird is an Iberian speciality, breeding throughout the peninsula from the foothills of the Pyrenees south to Tarifa and replacing the common Starling throughout this area. It is a typical urban bird, usually nesting in holes or crevices in buildings and is seldom found very far away from the influence of humans.

Elsewhere in Europe, the Spotless Starling is found only in Corsica, Sardinia and Sicily, but also breeds in North Africa. Surprisingly perhaps, it is a rare visitor to the Balearics. Flocks of common Starlings winter in Spain and the two species mix readily. It is quite simple to pick out the Spotless Starlings in the flock, because their lack of spots gives them a much darker appearance.

In recent years the Spotless Starling has been extending its breeding range. For example, it first bred on Gibraltar in the early 1960s but now the Rock has a breeding population of several hundred pairs; and it first nested in Cataluña in 1960 where many colonies are now established.

The spread northwards has also resulted in this species breeding on the French side of the Pyrenees with the first nesting place found there in 1990.

Spotless Starling

SPANISH SPARROW
Gorrión Moruno *Passer hispaniolensis*

Despite its name, the Spanish Sparrow is a rare bird in Iberia and its distribution is highly localized. In a few areas - particularly in Andalucíaand Extremadura - it may be quite abundant but it is absent from many areas where the habitat appears suitable and is a vagrant to much of northern Spain. Unlike the closely related House Sparrow, it is a rural bird and is seldom found in proximity to humans. Spanish Sparrows often nest in the base of the nests of White Storks and rural stork nests are often a likely place to look for this species.

Although an adult male Spanish Sparrow is easy to identify by its breeding plumage, it is much harder to spot in autumn, when the plumage more closely resembles that of a House Sparrow. The females of the two species are very similar. Iberian Spanish Sparrows are partial migrants, moving north through the Strait of Gibraltar in March and April, returning to North Africa from mid-July through to October though never in any numbers. It is quite likely that a few birds remain in Spain during the winter.

Spanish Sparrow

Rock Sparrow

ROCK SPARROW
Gorrión Chillón *Petronia petronia*
Drab and easy to overlook, the Rock Sparrow is a common bird throughout the upland areas of Iberia. This is the only European *Petronia*, but the distinctive yellow spot on the throat is often difficult to see. A better field mark is the broad, pale, supercilium which contrasts with the dark crown stripe.

As the name implies the Rock Sparrow favours rocky habitat and, though it ranges high into the foothills of the Pyrenees, it is not a true mountain bird and is just as likely to be encountered at lower altitudes. Favoured habitat ranges from cliffs to ruins and even buildings in towns. In winter, Rock Sparrows can often be found feeding in fields, sometimes in company with House Sparrows and smaller finches. Apart from local movements, they are sedentary birds.

CITRIL FINCH
Verdecillo Serrano *Serinus citrinella*
This is Europe's only endemic mountain bird, restricted in its range to the Alps, Corsica and Sardinia; and, in Spain, the Pyrenees, the Cantabrians and the Sierra de Guadarrama. It is a bird of alpine meadows and can be found from 1,200m right up to the treeline. Like most alpine birds it moves to lower altitudes in the winter and mixes freely with other finches.

Citril Finches are easy to overlook but the most obvious field marks are the unstreaked back of the adult male and the absence of any light-coloured patches in the wings and tail. However, the yellowish rump shows well when the birds fly away from you. Though these birds are invariably found close to pine forests they spend much of their time feeding on the ground, where they forage for grass and pine seeds.

Snowfinch

SNOWFINCH
Gorrión Alpino *Montifringilla nivalis*

Although a familiar bird to skiers in the Pyrenees during the winter, when flocks feed confidingly around alpine chalets and ski-lifts, it is much harder to find in the summer. As the snow melts, so the Snowfinches move up to the highest altitudes. Finding the birds is all the more difficult because of their excellent camouflage, their weak call notes and their reluctance to flush. They breed on rocky slopes and plateaux, well above the treeline.

Snowfinches are sedentary, their movements simply altitudinal in response to the seasons. They are extremely rare away from the Pyrenees or the Cantabrians, though during the last century they were recorded breeding in the Sierra Nevada.

SERIN
Verdecillo *Serinus serinus*
Despite its diminutive size, the Serin is not easily overlooked. From late winter onwards the cock starts his cheerful jingling song, delivered either from a perch or in an attractive display flight. Though Serins range widely and can commonly be found breeding in maquis, or even quite high in the mountains, they are most abundant around cultivated land as well as in gardens and parks.

Serins can be found in Iberia and the Balearics throughout the year, but many of the breeding birds move south to North Africa in the late autumn with wintering birds from central and western Europe taking their place, most of which winter close to the Mediterranean coast. Northward migration starts in early February, and peaks during the first half of March.

Serin

Crossbill

CROSSBILL
Piquituerto Común *Loxia curvirostra*
These birds are widely distributed in Iberia and breed in most mountain ranges where suitable pine and spruce woods can be found. In Iberia they tend to be birds of the mountains, less often seen at low altitudes, even where suitable habitat apparently exists. However, the eruptional habits of Crossbills ensure that isolated populations may occasionally become established in areas where they are seldom seen. These populations will flourish for a year or two and then suddenly disappear.

Crossbills are common breeding birds in the Balearics.

Though easily recognised when seen well, Crossbills often feed in the tops of trees, where they can be hard to see. Their flight call, a hard 'chip', frequently reveals their presence.

TRUMPETER FINCH
Camachuelo Trompetero *Bucanetes githagineus*
This species is a recent addition to the list of Spanish breeding birds - it was first presumed to be nesting in the deserts of Almería in 1968 and was

found breeding in the Cartagena Mountains in 1988. The most important area for this species is the Sierra Alhamilla - Campo de Níjar, where as many as 200 pairs nest within the deeply eroded gullies and dry wasteland.

Smaller populations have been found elsewhere in the region, including the Sierra del Cabo de Gata. These are the only known nesting populations in Europe. It is thought that the colonization of Spain is relatively recent, but it is possible that this species may well have been overlooked in the past.

Because of the harshness of their favoured terrain and their excellent camouflage, Trumpeter Finches are difficult to find. It is usually the male's distinctive song which draws the observer's attention, but even then the call can be difficult to pinpoint. The Spanish birds are migrants, returning to North Africa in the winter, but they are rarely recorded on passage.

Trumpeter Finch

HAWFINCH
Picogordo *Coccothraustes coccothraustes*

Although a scarce and localized breeding bird in the north of Iberia, the Hawfinch is much more common in the south and south-west, where it is a characteristic species of the cork oak woods. Even here it is easily overlooked, for it is a shy retiring bird. It is most frequently seen in flight. When seen flying, its bright white wing bars are obvious, while its explosive 'tic' call (not dissimilar to the alarm note of a Robin) frequently reveals its presence.

Most Hawfinches are probably sedentary but there is a regular passage of birds through the Strait of Gibraltar in March and early April, and then October and early November. It is not known whether these are local birds or from more distant populations.

Hawfinch

Cirl Bunting at nest

CIRL BUNTING
Escribano Soteño *Emberiza cirlus*

In Iberia, the Cirl Bunting fills a similar ecological role to that of the Yellowhammer in northern Europe. It is a bird of open, cultivated, country and favours a mixture of fields and gardens to forage in, and trees and hedges for cover. It ranges quite widely, being found in mountainous areas, as well as river valleys, and can be found anywhere where suitable conditions exist. Though an adult cock, with his distinctive stripy face pattern, is easy to recognise, the female and immature are more nondescript and resemble a female Yellowhammer. However, the latter is rarely found in the Mediterranean region.

Cirl Buntings are partial migrants: in the winter, numbers are augmented by wintering birds from farther north, possibly France, but there is little noticeable movement of birds to and from North Africa.

Rock Bunting

ROCK BUNTING
Escribano Montesino *Emberiza cia*

Cirl and Rock Buntings can occasionally be found side by side, but the latter is more a bird of the mountains, favouring stony slopes, preferably with a scattering of bushes. Widely distributed throughout Iberia, it is a common bird in many areas.

Unlike the Ortolan and Cirl Bunting, the sexes look similar, though the female Rock Bunting is a duller version of her mate.

Like the Cirl Bunting, the Rock Bunting is a partial migrant. Most birds are probably resident, but some birds from France are thought to move southwest to winter in Iberia.

ORTOLAN BUNTING
Escribano Hortelano *Emberiza hortulana*
The Ortolan is the only bunting to breed in the Iberian Peninsula which is exclusively a summer visitor. It is a late migrant - the first birds do not return until early April with peak passage in late April and early May. The Ortolan's autumn passage is concentrated mainly in September and early October. It winters in tropical Africa.

Although there is some overlap of habitat with the resident Cirl Bunting, the Ortolan's diet is more insectivorous and butterfly larvae form an important part. It likes open, cultivated, land with scattered trees for song posts. The cock's song is attractive and tuneful and is a good way of locating this species. In the south it is a mountain bird.

Ortolan Bunting at nest

CORN BUNTING
Triguero *Miliaria calandra*

In recent years many northern populations of Corn Buntings have declined, but this species remains an abundant breeding bird throughout much of Iberia. It is most numerous on the cereal-growing plains of central Spain, where during the spring scores of singing males can be counted on telegraph wires, delivering their simple song. However, roadside counts may give a distorted impression of numbers, as the cock requires an elevated song post to establish his territory, whereas Corn Buntings are generally absent from areas with no suitable bushes or telegraph poles for song posts.

In winter, Corn Buntings gather together into sizeable flocks, feeding in stubbles or on arable land. Some move south into Morocco, but the majority probably remain close to their breeding area.

Corn Bunting

OTHER BIRDS

WATERBIRDS AND SEABIRDS

Black-browed Albatross
Albatros Ojeroso *Diomedea melanophris*
An accidental visitor to Spain.

Wandering Albatross
Albatros Viajero *Diomedea exulans*
An accidental visitor to Portugal.

Fulmar
Fulmar *Fulmarus glacialis*
A scarce winter visitor to Atlantic, mainly northern, coastal areas of Spain and Portugal.

Bulwer's Petrel
Petrel de Bulwer *Bulweria bulwerii*
An accidental visitor.

Great Shearwater
Pardela Capirotada *Puffinus gravis*
A relatively scarce passage migrant along Atlantic coastal areas in autumn. An accidental to the Mediterranean coast.

Sooty Shearwater
Pardela Sombría *Puffinus griseus*
A regular autumn migrant in small numbers along Atlantic coastal areas with occasional entrances into the Strait of Gibraltar and the Mediterranean.

Little Shearwater
Pardela Chica *Puffinus assimilis*
An accidental visitor to Spanish Atlantic coastal areas, the Strait of Gibraltar and the Alboran Sea.

Masked Booby
Piquero Blanco *Sula dactylactra*
An accidental to Spain.

African Gannet
Alcatraz de El Cabo *Sula capensis*
An accidental to Spain.

Brown Booby
Piquero Pardo *Sula leucogaster*
An accidental to Spain.

Wilson's Petrel
Paiño de Wilson *Oceanites oceanicus*
A regular autumn migrant, in small numbers off Atlantic sectors.

Storm Petrel
Paiño Común *Hydrobates pelagicus*
Breeds in the Balearic Islands and the Columbretes Islands. Threatened as a breeding species. Occurs as a migrant along offshore areas, rarely coming close to the coast.

Madeiran Petrel
Paiño de Madeira *Oceanodroma castro*
A threatened breeding species on the Berlengas Islands, off the Portuguese coast. Accidental to Spain.

Leach's Petrel
Paiño de Leach *Oceanodroma leucorhoa*
A passage migrant in small numbers and a scarce winter visitor to Atlantic areas, rarely seen from land except when wrecked after gales. Accidental to the Balearic Islands.

Frigate Petrel
Paiño Pechialbo *Pelagodroma marina*
An accidental to the Portuguese coast.

Black-throated Diver
Colimbo Chico *Gavia stellata*
A very scarce winter visitor to Atlantic coastal areas. Accidental to the Balearic Islands.

Red-throated Diver
Colimbo Artico *Gavia arctica*
A scarce winter visitor, reaching the Strait of Gibraltar and adjacent Mediterranean areas. Accidental to the Balearic Islands.

Great Northern Diver
Colimbo Grande *Gavia immer*
A scarce winter visitor, reaching the Strait of Gibraltar. Accidental to the Balearic Islands.

White-billed Diver
Colimbo de Adams *Gavia adamsii*
An accidental to peninsular Spain.

Little Grebe
Zampullín Chico *Tachybaptus ruficollis*
A widely distributed resident with additional birds occurring on passage and as winter visitors.

Great Grebe
Somormujo Grande *Podiceps major*
An accidental to Spain.

Slavonian Grebe
Zampullín Cuelirrojo *Podiceps auritus*
An accidental visitor.

Red-necked Grebe
Somormujo Cuellirojo *Podiceps grisegena*
An accidental to peninsular Spain and the Balearic Islands.

Great Crested Grebe
Somormujo Lavanco *Podiceps cristatus*
A widely distributed resident, which receives additional numbers in winter.

Cormorant
Cormorán Grande *Phalacrocorax carbo*
An abundant migrant and winter visitor, especially along the Atlantic seaboard.

Pygmy Cormorant
Cormorán Pigmeo *Phalacrocorax pygmaeus*
An accidental to peninsular Spain.

Magnificent Frigatebird
Rabihorcado Grande *Fregata magnificens*
An accidental to peninsular Spain.

White Pelican
Pelícano Blanco *Pelecanus onocrotalus*
An accidental visitor to peninsular Spain and the Balearic Islands.

Grey Heron
Garza Real *Ardea cinerea*
A moderately abundant and well-distributed resident, whose numbers are greatly augmented by migrants during the winter.

Great White Egret
Garceta Grande *Egretta alba*
An accidental species.

Western Reef Heron
Garceta Dimorfa *Egretta gularis*
An accidental to peninsular Spain.

American Bittern
Avetoro Lentiginoso *Botaurus lentiginosus*
An accidental to peninsular Spain.

Bittern
Avetoro *Botaurus stellaris*
A resident which has seriously declined and is now in danger of extinction. Occurs as a scarce migrant and winter visitor.

Bald Ibis
Ibis Pelucón *Geronticus eremita*
An accidental to peninsular Spain.

Lesser Flamingo
Flamenco Enano *Phoenicopterus minor*
An accidental to peninsular Spain.

Fulvous Whistling Duck
Suirirí Leonado *Dendrocygna bicolor*
An accidental to peninsular Spain.

White-faced Whistling Duck
Suirirí Cariblanco *Dendrocygna viduata*
An accidental to peninsular Spain and the Balearic
Islands.

Mute Swan
Cisne Real *Cygnus olor*
An accidental visitor.

Whooper Swan
Cisne Cantor *Cygnus cygnus*
An accidental visitor.

Bewick's Swan
Cisne Chico *Cygnus bewickii*
An accidental to peninsular Spain and the Balearic
Islands.

Bean Goose
Ansar Campestre *Anser fabalis*
A fairly scarce winter visitor to the Iberian
Peninsula and an accidental to the Balearic
Islands.

Pink-footed Goose
Ansar Piquicorto *Anser brachyrhynchus*
An accidental to peninsular Spain.

White-fronted Goose
Ansar Careto Grande *Anser albifrons*
An accidental visitor.

Lesser White-fronted Goose
Ansar Careto Chico *Anser erythropus*
An accidental to peninsular Spain.

Bar-headed Goose
Ansar Indio *Anser indicus*
An accidental to peninsular Spain.

Snow Goose
Ansar Nival *Anser caerulescens*
An accidental to peninsular Spain.

Canada Goose
Barnacla Canadiense *Branta canadensis*
An accidental to peninsular Spain.

Barnacle Goose
Barnacla Cariblanca *Branta leucopsis*
A scarce winter visitor to peninsular Spain.

Brent Goose
Branta Carinegra *Branta bernicla*
A scarce winter visitor to the Iberian Peninsula.

Red-breasted Goose
Barnacla Cuelliroja *Branta ruficollis*
An accidental to peninsular Spain.

Egyptian Goose
Ganso del Nilo *Alopochen aegyptiacus*
An accidental to peninsular Spain.

Shelduck
Tarro Blanco *Tadorna tadorna*
A small breeding population which is in danger
of extinction. Winters widely, generally in small
numbers, and is scarce in the Balearic Islands.

Mandarin Duck
Pato Mandarín *Aix galericulata*
An accidental to peninsular Spain.

Wigeon
Anade Silbón *Anas penelope*
An abundant migrant and winter visitor.

American Wigeon
Anade Silbón Americano *Anas americana*
An accidental to peninsular Spain.

Gadwall
Anade Friso *Anas strepera*
A breeding species in small numbers but numbers
are largely increased during the winter.

Teal
Cerceta Común *Anas crecca*
An abundant winter visitor.

Baikal Teal
Cerceta de Baikal *Anas formosa*
An accidental to peninsular Spain.

Mallard
Anade Real *Anas platyrhynchos*
A common and widely distributed breeding species, and an abundant winter visitor.

Pintail
Anade Rabudo *Anas acuta*
An abundant winter visitor.

Blue-winged Teal
Cerceta Aliazul *Anas discors*
An accidental visitor.

Shoveler
Pato Cuchara *Anas clypeata*
An abundant winter visitor.

Pochard
Porrón Común *Aythya ferina*
Breeds in moderate numbers and is an abundant winter visitor.

Tufted Duck
Porrón Moñudo *Aythya fuligula*
An abundant winter visitor.

Scaup
Porrón Bastardo *Aythya marila*
A very scarce winter visitor to northern Spain and an accidental elsewhere.

Ring-necked Duck
Porrón de Collar *Aythya collaris*
An accidental to peninsular Spain.

Eider
Eider *Somateria mollissima*
A regular winter visitor to the Cantabrian and Catalan coasts and an accidental visitor elsewhere.

Long-tailed Duck
Havelda *Clangula hyemalis*
A very rare visitor.

Common Scoter
Negrón Común *Melanitta nigra*
An abundant migrant and winter visitor to coastal areas. Accidental to the Balearic Islands.

Velvet Scoter
Negrón Especulado *Melanitta fusca*
A regular winter visitor to the Cantabrian and Catalan coasts and an accidental visitor elsewhere.

Surf Scoter
Negron Careto *Melanitta perspicillata*
An accidental to peninsular Spain.

Goldeneye
Porrón Osculado *Bucephala clangula*
A very scarce winter visitor, even south to Andalucía.

Barrow's Goldeneye
Porrón Islándico *Bucephala islandica*
An accidental to peninsular Spain.

Smew
Serreta Chica *Mergus albellus*
An accidental visitor.

Red-breasted Merganser
Serreta Mediana *Mergus serrator*
A winter visitor in moderate numbers.

Goosander
Serreta Grande *Mergus merganser*
An accidental to peninsular Spain.

Ruddy Duck
Malvasia Canela *Oxyura jamaicensis*
An increasingly frequent visitor which, if established, may become a serious threat to the survival of the White-headed Duck.

Water Rail
Rascón *Rallus aquaticus*
A resident of Iberian wetlands in moderate numbers having declined considerably because of loss of habitat. Numbers increase in winter due to migrants arriving from the north.

Spotted Crake
Polluela Pintoja *Porzana porzana*
A migrant that is often overlooked and which appears to have declined in numbers. It may breed in some Spanish wetlands, but this requires confirmation.

Little Crake
Polluela Bastarda *Porzana parva*
A moderately common migrant and winter visitor.

Sora Rail
Polluela de la Carolina *Porzana carolina*
An accidental to peninsular Spain.

Corncrake
Guión *Crex crex*
A scarce passage migrant to the Iberian Peninsula, where it has bred, and accidental to the Balearic Islands.

Moorhen
Polla de Agua *Gallinula chloropus*
A common resident species with increases during passage and in the winter.

Allen's Gallinule
Calamón Chico *Porphyrula alleni*
An accidental to the Iberian Peninsula.

Coot
Focha Común *Fulica atra*
An abundant and widely distributed resident, migrant and winter visitor.

Demoiselle Crane
Grulla Damisela *Anthropoides virgo*
An accidental to the Iberian Peninsula and the Balearic Islands.

Brunnich's Guillemot
Arao de Brunnich *Uria lomvia*
Accidental to peninsular Spain.

Razorbill
Alca *Alca torda*
An abundant migrant and winter visitor.

Little Auk
Mérgulo Marino *Alle alle*
A scarce winter visitor, which occasionally reaches south to the Strait of Gibraltar.

Puffin
Frailecillo *Fratercula arctica*
An abundant migrant and winter visitor.

BIRDS OF PREY

White-tailed Eagle
Pigargo Coliblanco *Haliaetus albicilla*
An accidental to the Iberian Peninsula.

Pallid Harrier
Aguilucho *Papialbo Circus macrourus*
An accidental visitor to peninsular Spain and the Balearic Islands.

Dark Chanting Goshawk
Azor Lagartijero *Melierax metabates*
An accidental to peninsular Spain.

Sparrowhawk
Gavilan *Accipiter nisus*
A resident species whose numbers are greatly increased by migrants during the passage periods, as well as in the winter.

Buzzard
Ratonero Común *Buteo buteo*
A common resident. An abundant migrant and winter visitor.

Long-legged Buzzard
Ratonero Moro *Buteo rufinus*
An accidental to peninsular Spain.

Rough-legged Buzzard
Ratonero Calzado *Buteo lagopus*
An accidental to peninsular Spain and the Balearic Islands.

Lesser Spotted Eagle
Aguila Pomerana *Aquila pomarina*
An accidental visitor.

Spotted Eagle
Aguila Moteada *Aquila clanga*
An accidental visitor.

Tawny Eagle
Aguila Rapaz *Aquila rapax*
An accidental to peninsular Spain.

Red-footed Falcon
Cernícalo Patirrojo *Falco vespertinus*
A very scarce migrant in the spring.

Merlin

Esmerejón *Falco columbarius*
A regular winter visitor, which is more abundant in the northern half of Iberia with smaller numbers reaching, and crossing, the Strait of Gibraltar. An accidental visitor to the Balearic Islands.

Hobby

Alcotán *Falco subbuteo*
A summer visitor with a reduced breeding population. West European birds are regular on passage.

Lanner

Halcón Borní *Falco biarmicus*
An accidental to peninsular Spain, where it may breed occasionally, and the Balearic Islands. A scarce, but fairly regular, migrant across the Strait of Gibraltar.

Gyr Falcon

Halcón Gerifalte *Falco rusticolus*
An accidental visitor.

LAND BIRDS

Ptarmigan

Perdiz Nival *Lagopus mutus*
A resident of the mountain regions of northern Spain.

Grey Partridge

Perdiz Pardilla *Perdix perdix*
A resident of northern areas of Spain and Portugal.

Pheasant

Faisán *Phasianus colchicus*
An introduced species, resident and widespread in peninsular Iberia and the Balearic Islands.

Houbara

Hubara *Chlamydotis undulata*
An accidental to peninsular Spain.

Pallas's Sandgrouse

Ganga de Pallas *Syrrhaptes paradoxus*
An accidental to peninsular Spain.

Rock Dove

Paloma Bravía *Columba livia*
An abundant resident species in rocky areas, from high sierras to coastal cliffs.

Stock Dove

Paloma Zurita *Columba oenas*
A localized resident species with increasing numbers in winter as migrants arrive from the north. Accidental to the Balearic Islands.

Wood Pigeon

Paloma Torcaz *Columba palumbus*
A well distributed and, in places, abundant resident. A very abundant winter visitor, especially to areas of western and southwestern Iberia.

African Collared Dove

Tórtola Rosigrís *Streptopelia roseogrisea*
Accidental to the Balearic Islands.

Collared Dove

Tórtola Turca *Streptopelia decaocto*
A resident in areas of northern Iberia, which is apparently slowly spreading southwards.

Turtle Dove

Tórtola Común *Streptopelia turtur*
An abundant and widely distributed breeding species and an abundant migrant.

Cuckoo

Cuco *Cuculus canorus*
An abundant and widely distributed breeding species, and an abundant migrant, particularly in the spring.

Barn Owl

Lechuza *Tyto alba*
An abundant and widely distributed resident with additional small numbers arriving in winter.

Pygmy Owl

Mochuelo Chico *Glaucidium passerinum*
An accidental to peninsular Spain.

Tawny Owl

Cárabo Común *Strix aluco*
A widely distributed, and in some areas, abundant resident.

Long-eared Owl
Búho Chico *Asio otus*
A locally common resident, with small numbers arriving from the north in the winter.

Short-eared Owl
Búho Campestre *Asio flammeus*
An abundant migrant and winter visitor.

African Marsh Owl
Búho Moro *Asio capensis*
An accidental to the Iberian Peninsula.

Tengmalm's Owl
Búho de Tengmalm *Aegolius funereus*
A localized resident in the Spanish Pyrenees.

Nightjar
Chotacabras Gris *Caprimulgus europaeus*
A locally common breeding species and an abundant migrant.

Needle-tailed Swift
Rabitojo Mongol *Hirundapus caudacutus*
An accidental to peninsular Spain.

Swift
Vencejo Común *Apus apus*
An abundant migrant and breeding species.

Little Swift
Vencejo Culiblanco *Apus affinis*
An accidental to peninsular Spain.

Kingfisher
Martín Pescador *Alcedo atthis*
A well distributed breeding species and an abundant winter visitor.

Blue-cheeked Bee-eater
Abejaruco Papirrojo *Merops superciliosus*
An accidental to peninsular Spain and Gibraltar.

Lesser Spotted Woodpecker
Pico Menor *Dendrocopos minor*
A localised resident.

Great Spotted Woodpecker
Pico Picapinos *Dendrocopos major*
An abundant and widely distributed resident.

WADERS, GULLS AND TERNS

Oystercatcher
Ostrero *Haematopus ostralegus*
Small numbers breed. Otherwise an abundant migrant and winter visitor, especially to Atlantic coastal areas. A scarce migrant in the Balearic Islands.

Cream-coloured Courser
Corredor *Cursorius cursor*
An accidental to the Iberian Peninsula and the Balearic Islands.

Black-winged Pratincole
Canastera Alinegra *Glareola nordmanni*
An accidental to peninsular Spain.

Little Ringed Plover
Chorlitejo Chico *Charadrius dubius*
An abundant migrant and summer visitor. Small numbers remain in winter.

Ringed Plover
Chorlitejo Grande *Charadrius hiaticula*
Has bred in northeastern Spain. Otherwise an abundant migrant and winter visitor, scarcer in the Balearic Islands.

Lesser Sand Plover
Chorlitejo Mongol Chico *Charadrius mongolus*
An accidental to peninsular Spain.

Semipalmated Plover
Chorlitejo Semipalmeado *Charadrius semipalmatus*
An accidental to peninsular Spain.

Dotterel
Chorlito Carambolo *Eudromias morinellus*
A relatively scarce migrant mainly across central Spain. A scarce winter visitor. Accidental to the Balearic Islands.

American Golden Plover
Chorlito Dorado Chico *Pluvialis dominica*
An accidental to peninsular Spain.

Golden Plover
Chorlito Dorado *Pluvialis apricaria*
An abundant migrant and winter visitor, scarce in the Balearic Islands.

Grey Plover
Chorlito Gris *Pluvialis squatarola*
An abundant migrant and winter visitor, scarce in the Balearic Islands.

Sociable Plover
Avefría Social *Chettusia gregaria*
An accidental to the Iberian Peninsula.

Spur-winged Plover
Avefría Espolonada *Vanellus spinosus*
An accidental visitor to peninsular Spain.

Lapwing
Avefría *Vanellus vanellus*
A localized breeding species, and an abundant migrant and winter visitor, particularly in cold winters.

Great Knot
Correlimos Grande *Calidris tenuirostris*
An accidental to peninsular Spain.

Knot
Correlimos Gordo *Calidris canutus*
A common migrant but scarce winter visitor to the Iberian Peninsula. Accidental to the Balearic Islands.

Sanderling
Correlimos Tridáctilo *Calidris alba*
An abundant migrant and a locally abundant winter visitor. Generally scarce in the Balearic Islands.

Little Stint
Correlimos Menudo *Calidris minuta*
An abundant migrant and scarce winter visitor.

Temminck's Stint
Correlimos de Temminck *Calidris temminckii*
A scarce migrant.

Western Sandpiper
Correlimos de Maur *Calidris mauri*
An accidental to peninsular Spain.

White-rumped Sandpiper
Correlimos de Bonaparte *Calidris fuscicollis*
An accidental to peninsular Spain and the Balearic Islands.

Pectoral Sandpiper
Correlimos Pectoral *Calidris melanotos*
An accidental to the Iberian Peninsula and the Balearic Islands.

Curlew Sandpiper
Correlimos Zarapitin *Calidris ferruginea*
An abundant migrant, scarcer in the Balearic Islands, and rare winter visitor.

Purple Sandpiper
Correlimos Oscuro *Calidris maritima*
A scarce migrant and winter visitor to the Iberian Peninsula, right down to the shores of the Strait of Gibraltar.

Dunlin
Correlimos Común *Calidris alpina*
An abundant migrant and winter visitor.

Stilt Sandpiper
Correlimos Zancolín *Micropalama himantopus*
An accidental to the Balearic Islands.

Broad-billed Sandpiper
Correlimos Falcinelo *Limicola falcinellus*
An accidental to the Iberian Peninsula.

Buff-breasted Sandpiper
Correlimos Canelo *Tryngites subruficollis*
An accidental to peninsular Spain.

Ruff
Combatiente *Philomachus pugnax*
An abundant migrant and scarce winter visitor.

Jack Snipe
Agachadiza Chica *Lymnocryptes minimus*
A fairly common migrant, probably often overlooked, and a scarce winter visitor.

Snipe
Agachadiza Común *Gallinago gallinago*
A resident in northwestern Iberia. Otherwise an abundant migrant and winter visitor.

Great Snipe
Agachadiza Real *Gallinago media*
An accidental to the Iberian Peninsula and the Balearic Islands.

Short-billed Dowitcher
Agujeta Gris *Limnodromus griseus*
An accidental to peninsular Spain.

Long-billed Dowitcher
Agujeta Escolopácea *Limnodromus scolopaceus*
An accidental to peninsular Spain.

Woodcock
Becada *Scolopax rusticola*
Resident in certain areas of northern Spain. An abundant winter visitor.

Black-tailed Godwit
Aguja Colinegra *Limosa limosa*
An abundant migrant and winter visitor.

Bar-tailed Godwit
Aguja Colipinta *Limosa lapponica*
An abundant migrant and winter visitor, mainly to Atlantic coastal areas. Accidental to the Balearic Islands.

Whimbrel
Zarapito Trinador *Numenius phaeopus*
An abundant migrant with smaller numbers remaining to winter. A scarcer migrant in the Balearic Islands.

Slender-billed Curlew
Zarapito Fino *Numenius tenuirostris*
A very rare migrant.

Curlew
Zarapito Real *Numenius arquata*
An abundant migrant and winter visitor, scarcer in the Balearic Islands.

Spotted Redshank
Archibebe Oscuro *Tringa erythropus*
A regular, at times abundant, migrant with very small numbers remaining in winter.

Redshank
Archibebe Común *Tringa totanus*
An abundant migrant and winter visitor, with a small breeding population mainly in the west.

Marsh Sandpiper
Archibebe Fino *Tringa stagnatilis*
A scarce migrant and occasional winter visitor.

Greenshank
Archibebe Claro *Tringa nebularia*
A regular migrant, usually in small numbers, with a small wintering population.

Lesser Yellowlegs
Archibebe Patigualdo Chico *Tringa flavipes*
An accidental to peninsular Spain.

Solitary Sandpiper
Andarríos Solitario *Tringa solitaria*
An accidental to peninsular Spain.

Green Sandpiper
Andarríos Grande *Tringa ochropus*
A regular, and in places abundant, migrant with a small wintering population.

Wood Sandpiper
Andarríos Bastardo *Tringa glareola*
A regular migrant, generally scarcer than the Green Sandpiper.

Terek Sandpiper
Andarríos de Terek *Xenus cinereus*
An accidental to peninsular Spain.

Common Sandpiper
Andarríos Chico *Actitis hypoleucos*
An abundant migrant and a regular winter visitor with a small breeding population.

Spotted Sandpiper
Andarríos Maculado *Actitis macularia*
An accidental to peninsular Spain.

Turnstone
Vuelvepiedras *Arenaria interpres*
An abundant migrant and a regular winter visitor to rocky coasts, mainly on the Atlantic coasts.

Wilson's Phalarope
Falaropo de Wilson *Phalaropus tricolor*
An accidental to peninsular Spain.

Red-necked Phalarope
Falaropo Picofino *Phalaropus lobatus*
A scarce migrant to peninsular Spain but regarded as accidental only to Portugal.

Grey Phalarope
Falaropo Picogrueso *Phalaropus fulicarius*
A regular migrant, usually in small numbers but occasionally wrecked in larger quantities, along coastal areas.

Pomarine Skua
Págalo Pomerano *Stercorarius pomarinus*
A regular migrant in small numbers.

Arctic Skua
Págalo Parasito *Stercorarius parasiticus*
A regular and common migrant which winters in small numbers.

Long-tailed Skua
Págalo Rabero *Stercorarius longicaudus*
A scarce migrant.

Great Skua
Págalo Grande *Stercorarius skua*
An abundant migrant and winter visitor with smaller numbers remaining throughout the summer.

Laughing Gull
Gaviota Reidora Americana *Larus atricilla*
An accidental to peninsular Iberia.

Franklin's Gull
Gaviota de Franklin *Larus pipixcan*
An accidental to peninsular Spain.

Little Gull
Gaviota Enana *Larus minutus*
An abundant migrant and winter visitor in small numbers to coastal areas. Larger wintering flocks are observed in the Mediterranean and the Strait of Gibraltar after stormy weather.

Sabine's Gull
Gaviota de Sabine *Larus sabini*
A scarce migrant off Atlantic coastal areas, occasionally straying into the Strait of Gibraltar.

Black-headed Gull
Gaviota Reidora *Larus ridibundus*
Breeds in peninsular Spain in relatively small and scattered groups. A very abundant migrant and winter visitor.

Bonaparte's Gull
Gaviota de Bonaparte *Larus philadelphia*
An accidental to peninsular Spain.

Grey-headed Gull
Gaviota Cabecigrís *Larus cirrocephalus*
An accidental to peninsular Spain.

Ring-billed Gull
Gaviota de Delaware *Larus delawarensis*
An accidental to the Iberian Peninsula.

Common Gull
Gaviota Cana *Larus canus*
A scarce migrant and winter visitor, mainly to Atlantic coastal areas.

Lesser black-backed Gull
Gaviota Sombría *Larus fuscus*
Breeds in small numbers in western and north-western Iberia. A very abundant migrant and winter visitor.

Herring Gull
Gaviota Argentea *Larus argentatus*
A migrant and winter visitor in small numbers, mainly to coastal areas of the Atlantic.

Iceland Gull
Gaviota Polar *Larus glaucoides*
An accidental to the Iberian Peninsula.

Glaucous Gull
Gaviota Hiperbórea *Larus hyperboreus*
An accidental to the Iberian Peninsula.

Great black-backed Gull
Gavión *Larus marinus*
A scarce winter visitor to peninsular Iberia. Accidental to the Balearic Islands.

Kittiwake
Gaviota Tridactila *Rissa tridactyla*
Breeds in small numbers in northwestern Atlantic areas. An abundant winter visitor.

Sandwich Tern
Charrán Patinegro *Sterna sandvicensis*
An abundant migrant and winter visitor, reaching
Gibraltar from colonies in the North Atlantic and
the Black Sea.

Roseate Tern
Charrán Rosado *Sterna dougallii*
A scarce migrant.

Common Tern
Charrán Común *Sterna hirundo*
A scarce breeding species in peninsular Spain. An
abundant migrant and a scarce wintering species.

Arctic Tern
Charrán Artico *Sterna paradisea*
A scarce migrant.

Sooty Tern
Charrán Sombrío *Sterna fuscata*
An accidental to peninsular Spain.

Little Tern
Charrancito *Sterna albifrons*
An abundant breeding species in suitable habitat,
principally saltmarshes and salt pans but with a
declining population. A regular migrant.

Black Tern
Fumarel Común *Chlidonias nigra*
A threatened breeding species with localized
populations. An abundant migrant and scarce
wintering species.

White-winged Black Tern
Fumarel Aliblanco *Chlidonias leucoptera*
A scarce migrant to peninsular Spain and an
accidental elsewhere.

SONGBIRDS

Hoopoe Lark
Alondra Ibis *Alaemon alaudipes*
An accidental to peninsular Spain.

Woodlark
Totovía *Lullula arborea*
A widely distributed, and in places abundant,
resident. A migrant and winter visitor in moderate
numbers.

Skylark
Alondra Común *Alauda arvensis*
A localised breeding species usually in mountain
peaks. An abundant migrant and winter visitor.

Shore Lark
Alondra Cornuda *Eremophila alpestris*
An accidental to peninsular Spain

Temminck's Horned Lark
Alondra Cornuda Cariblanca *Eremophila bilopha*
An accidental to peninsular Spain.

Sand Martin
Avión Zapador *Riparia riparia*
A widely distributed breeding species and a
common migrant.

Swallow
Golondrina Común *Hirundo rustica*
An abundant breeding species and migrant.
Occasional individuals are found in winter in the
south.

House Martin
Avión Comun *Delichon urbica*
An abundant breeding species and migrant.
Occasional individuals are found in winter in the
south.

Richard's Pipit
Bisbita Patilargo *Anthus novaseelandiae*
An accidental to the Iberian Peninsula and the
Balearics.

Tree Pipit
Bisbita Arbóreo *Anthus trivialis*
A breeding species in northern Spain and an
abundant migrant throughout.

Meadow Pipit
Bisbita Común *Anthus pratensis*
A very abundant migrant and winter visitor.

Red-throated Pipit
Bisbita Gorgirrojo *Anthus cervinus*
A scarce migrant to peninsular Spain and an accidental elsewhere.

Water Pipit
Bisbita Ribereño *Anthus spinoletta*
Breeds in high sierras in central and northern Spain. Otherwise a regular migrant and winter visitor, nowhere numerous.

Olive-backed Pipit
Bisbita de Hodgson *Anthus hodgsoni*
An accidental in the Balearic Islands.

Grey Wagtail
Lavandera Cascadeña *Motacilla cinerea*
A common and widespread breeding species. Numbers are augmented by wintering birds from the north.

White Wagtail
Lavandera Blanca *Motacilla alba*
A well distributed breeding species except in the south. An abundant migrant and winter visitor.

Citrine Wagtail
Lavandera Cetrina *Motacilla citreola*
An accidental to peninsular Spain

Common Bulbul
Bulbul Naranjero *Pycnonotus barbatus*
An accidental to peninsular Spain.

Waxwing
Ampelis *Bombycilla garrulus*
An accidental to the Iberian Peninsula.

Dipper
Mirlo Acuático *Cinclus cinclus*
A localized resident, mainly along mountain streams.

Wren
Chochín *Troglodytes troglodytes*
An abundant and widely dispersed resident.

Dunnock
Acentor Común *Prunella modularis*
A resident species in northern areas and a regular migrant and winter visitor, usually in small numbers, elsewhere.

Robin
Petirrojo *Erithacus rubecula*
A common and widespread resident in woodland. A very abundant migrant and winter visitor.

Redstart
Colirrojo Real *Phoenicurus phoenicurus*
A localized breeding species. An abundant migrant.

Whinchat
Tarabilla Norteña *Saxicola rubetra*
Breeds in the north of the Iberian Peninsula. Elsewhere it is an abundant migrant.

Isabelline Wheatear
Collalba Isabel *Oenanthe isabellina*
An accidental to peninsular Spain.

Wheatear
Collalba Gris *Oenanthe oenanthe*
A localized breeding species, typical of mountain peaks, and an abundant migrant.

Desert Wheatear
Collalba Desértica *Oenanthe deserti*
An accidental to peninsular Spain and Gibraltar.

White-crowned Black Wheatear
Collalba Yebélica *Oenanthe leucopyga*
An accidental to peninsular Spain.

White's Thrush
Zorzal Dorado *Zoothera dauma*
An accidental to the Balearic Islands.

Blackbird
Mirlo Común *Turdus merula*
An abundant and widespread resident, and a migrant and winter visitor in small numbers.

Black-throated Thrush
Zorzal Papirrojo y Papinegro *Turdus ruficollis*
An accidental to peninsular Spain.

Fieldfare
Zorzal Real *Turdus pilaris*
A regular winter visitor, especially to northern areas.

Song Thrush
Zorzal Común *Turdus philomelos*
Breeds in northern Spain. A very abundant migrant and winter visitor throughout.

Redwing
Zorzal Alirrojo *Turdus iliacus*
An abundant migrant and winter visitor.

Mistle Thrush
Zorzal Charlo *Turdus viscivorus*
An abundant and widespread resident with increasing numbers during the winter.

Grasshopper Warbler
Buscarla Pintoja *Locustella naevia*
Breeds in northern Spain, generally in small numbers. A regular migrant which is nowhere numerous.

River Warbler
Buscarla Fluvial *Locustella fluviatilis*
An accidental to peninsular Spain.

Aquatic Warbler
Carricerín Cejudo *Acrocephalus paludicola*
A scarce migrant to peninsular Spain and an accidental to the Balearic Islands.

Sedge Warbler
Carricerín Común *Acrocephalus schoenobaenus*
A very scarce and localized breeding species in northern Spain. A regular and abundant migrant.

Blyth's Reed Warbler
Carricero de Blyth *Acrocephalus dumetorum*
An accidental to peninsular Spain and Gibraltar.

Marsh Warbler
Carricero Políglota *Acrocephalus palustris*
A scarce migrant and an accidental to the Balearic islands.

Reed Warbler
Carricero Común *Acrocephalus scirpaceus*
A localized, but in places common, breeding species. An abundant migrant.

Olive-tree Warbler
Zarcero Grande *Hippolais olivetorum*
An accidental to peninsular Spain.

Icterine Warbler
Zarcero Icterino *Hippolais icterina*
A scarce migrant.

Tristram's Warbler
Curruca de Tristram *Sylvia deserticola*
An accidental to Gibraltar.

Menetries's Warbler
Curruca de Menetries *Sylvia mystacea*
An accidental to the Iberian Peninsula.

Barred Warbler
Curruca Gavilana *Sylvia nisoria*
An accidental to peninsular Spain and the Balearic Islands.

Lesser Whitethroat
Curruca Zarcerilla *Sylvia curruca*
A very scarce migrant across peninsular Spain and an accidental elsewhere.

Whitethroat
Curruca Zarcera *Sylvia communis*
An abundant and widespread breeding species. An abundant migrant.

Garden Warbler
Curruca Mosquitera *Sylvia borin*
An abundant and widely dispersed breeding species in northern Iberia. An abundant migrant throughout.

Blackcap
Curruca Capirotada *Sylvia atricapilla*
A widespread and abundant resident with large increases in numbers during migration and in the winter.

Greenish Warbler
Mosquitero Troquiloide *Phylloscopus trochiloides*
An accidental to Spain.

Yellow-browed Warbler
Mosquitero Bilistado *Phylloscopus inornatus*
An accidental to the Iberian Peninsula.

Radde's Warbler
Mosquitero de Schwarz *Phylloscopus schwarzi*
An accidental to peninsular Spain.

Dusky Warbler
Mosquitero Sombrio *Phylloscopus fuscatus*
An accidental to Gibraltar and Portugal.

Wood Warbler
Mosquitero Silbador *Phylloscopus sibilatrix*
A localized breeding species in northern Spain. A scarce migrant, which is most numerous in the spring.

Chiffchaff
Mosquitero Común *Phylloscopus collybita*
A well-distributed resident and an abundant migrant and winter visitor.

Willow Warbler
Mosquitero Musical *Phylloscopus trochilus*
A well-distributed breeding species in northern Spain and a very abundant migrant elsewhere.

Goldcrest
Reyezuelo Sencillo *Regulus regulus*
A localized breeding species on central Spanish and Pyrenean mountains. A regular migrant and winter visitor.

Spotted Flycatcher
Papamoscas Gris *Muscicapa striata*
A widespread and abundant migrant and breeding species.

Red-breasted Flycatcher
Papamoscas Papirrojo *Ficedula parva*
An accidental to peninsular Spain.

Collared Flycatcher
Papamoscas Collarino *Ficedula albicollis*
A very scarce migrant across peninsular Spain and an accidental elsewhere.

Pied Flycatcher
Papamoscas Cerrojillo *Ficedula hypoleuca*
A well-dispersed and, in places, common breeding species and an abundant migrant.

Bearded Tit
Bigotudo *Panurus biarmicus*
A localized breeding species in peninsular Spain and an accidental to Portugal.

Long-tailed Tit
Mito *Aegithalos caudatus*
An abundant and well-distributed resident.

Marsh Tit
Carbonero Palustre *Parus palustris*
A localised breeding species of northern Spanish woods and is an accidental elsewhere.

Coal Tit
Carbonero Garrapinos *Parus ater*
An abundant resident, typical of woods in the north and of mountainous woodland in the south.

Blue Tit
Herrerillo Común *Parus caeruleus*
An abundant and widespread resident with increases in winter due to the arrival of migrants.

Great Tit
Carbonero Común *Parus major*
An abundant and widespread resident, with increases in winter due to the arrival of migrants.

Nuthatch
Trepador Común *Sitta europaea*
A localized resident.

Tree Creeper
Agateador Norteño *Certhia familiaris*
A localized resident in the north.

Masked Shrike
Alcaudón Enmascarado *Lanius nubicus*
An accidental to peninsular Spain.

Jay
Arrendajo Común *Garrulus glandarius*
A well-distributed and abundant resident.

Magpie
Urraca *Pica pica*
A widely distributed and abundant resident, except in the extreme south and the Balearic Islands.

Nutcracker
Cascanueces *Nucifraga caryocatactes*
An accidental to the Iberian Peninsula.

Jackdaw
Grajilla *Corvus monedula*
An abundant and widely distributed resident.

Rook
Graja *Corvus frugilegus*
A localized resident of northern Spain. Numbers are augmented by wintering birds.

Carrion Crow
Corneja Negra *Corvus corone*
A well-distributed and relatively abundant resident of central and northern Spain, with small numbers reaching the south in the winter.

Starling
Estornino Pinto *Sturnus vulgaris*
A localized resident species in northern Spain, but an abundant winter visitor throughout.

Rose-coloured Starling
Estornino Rosado *Sturnus roseus*
An accidental to the Iberian Peninsula.

House Sparrow
Gorrión Común *Passer domesticus*
A widespread and abundant resident.

Tree Sparrow
Gorrión Molinero *Passer montanus*
An abundant and well distributed resident, with numbers increasing in winter with the arrival of birds from the north.

Chaffinch
Pinzón Común *Fringilla coelebs*
An abundant and well-dispersed resident. A very abundant migrant and winter visitor.

Brambling
Pinzón Real *Fringilla montifringilla*
A regular winter visitor, especially frequent in the north and least so in the south.

Greenfinch
Verderón *Carduelis chloris*
An abundant and widely distributed resident. A very abundant migrant and winter visitor.

Goldfinch
Jilguero *Carduelis carduelis*
A very abundant and widely dispersed resident. A very abundant migrant and winter visitor.

Siskin
Lúgano *Carduelis spinus*
Breeds in the Pyrenees. Elsewhere a winter visitor, sometimes in large numbers.

Linnet
Pardillo Común *Acanthis cannabina*
An abundant and well-dispersed resident. A very abundant migrant and winter visitor.

Twite
Pardillo Piquigualdo *Acanthis flavirostris*
An accidental to the Iberian Peninsula.

Redpoll
Pardillo Sizerín *Acanthis flammea*
An accidental to the Iberian Peninsula.

Scarlet Rosefinch
Camachuelo Carminoso *Carpodacus erythrinus*
An accidental to Spain.

Bullfinch
Camachuelo Común *Pyrrhula pyrrhula*
A localized resident in the north. Reaches further south, rarely down to the Strait of Gibraltar, in the winter.

Rose-breasted Grosbeak
Candelo Tricolor *Pheuticus ludovicianus*
An accidental to peninsular Spain.

Lapland Bunting
Escribano Lapón *Calcarius lapponicus*
An accidental to the Iberian Peninsula.

Pine Bunting
Escribano de Gámelin *Emberiza leucocephalos*
An accidental to peninsular Spain and Gibraltar.

Yellowhammer
Escribano Cerillo *Emberiza citrinella*
A localized breeding species in the north and a
scarce winter visitor further south, rarely reaching
the Strait of Gibraltar.

Little Bunting
Escribano Pigmeo *Emberiza pusilla*
An accidental to peninsular Spain.

Yellow-breasted Bunting
Escribano Aureolado *Emberiza aureola*
An accidental to peninsular Spain.

Reed Bunting
Escribano Palustre *Emberiza schoeniclus*
A localized resident, with numbers significantly
augmented in winter.

Red-headed Bunting
Escribano Carirrojo *Emberiza bruniceps*
An accidental to peninsular Spain.

Black-headed Bunting
Escribano Cabecinegro *Emberiza melanocephala*
An accidental to peninsular Spain and the Balearic
Islands.

Snow Bunting
Escribano Nival *Plectrophenax nivalis*
A very scarce winter visitor and an accidental to
the Balearic Islands.

White-throated Sparrow
Chingolo Gorgiblanco *Zonotrichia albicollis*
An accidental to Gibraltar.

Slate-coloured Junco
Junco Pizarroso *Junco hyemalis*
An accidental to Gibraltar.

INDEX OF BIRDS

✦ B ✦

C

✦ D ✦

O

P

T

U

V

W

X

Y

Z

GEOGRAPHICAL INDEX

FURTHER READING

Cramp, Stanley. *The Birds of the Western Palaearctic.* Oxford University Press, 1977.

del Hoy, J. et al. *Where to Watch Birds in Catalonia,* Lynx, 1989.

Finlayson, Clive. *Birds of the Strait of Gibraltar.* Poyser, 1992.

Génsbol, Benny. *Birds of Prey of Britain and Europe.* Collins, 1984.

Grimmett, R.F.A. and Jones, T.A. *Important Bird Areas in Europe.* ICBP, 1989.

Jonsson, Lars. *Birds of the Mediterranean and Alps.* Croom Helm, 1982.

Lewington, Ian et al. *A Field Guide to the Rare Birds of Britain and Europe.* Harper Collins, 1991.

Mountford, Guy. *Portrait of a Wilderness.* Hutchinson, 1958.

MORE GREAT BOOKS
ON SPAIN

Excursions in Southern Spain
by David Baird. 280 pages

Forty great trips through Andalusia, from the premier travel writer in Spain today. Here, at last, is a handy guided tour of Spain's most fascinating region, packed with practical information, interesting facts, tips on where to eat and where to stay, and clear maps.

The Story of Spain
by Mark Williams. 272 pages

The bold and dramatic history of Spain, from the caves of Altamira to our day. This is a story of kings and poets, saints and conquistadores, of Torquemada, Picasso, Cervantes, Franco, the Alhambra, the Escorial… Mark Williams has drawn on years of rigorous research to re-create the drama, excitement and pathos of crucial events in the history of the western world. Illustrated in colour.

Gardening in Spain
by Marcelle Pitt. 216 pages

Your most valuable tool for successful gardening in Spain, from the author of Lookout magazines's popular gardening column. How to plan your garden, what to plant, when and how to plant it, how to make the most of flowers, trees, shrubs, herbs. Illustrated with full-colour photographs.

Cooking in Spain
by Janet Mendel. 376 pages

The definitive guide to cooking in Spain, with more than 400 great Spanish recipes. Plus complete information on Spain's regional specialities and culinary history, how to buy the best at the market, a complete English-Spanish glossary with more than 500 culinary terms, handy conversion guide… all of it illustrated with colour photographs.

Spanish Property Owners' Handbook
by David Searl. 100 pages

Do you know your rights and obligations as a member of your community of property owners? Here, at last, are the answers! Including full text, in Spanish and English, of the Ley de la propiedad horizontal, with comments by legal writer David Searl.

The Best of Spanish Cooking
by Janet Mendel. 172 pages

The top food writer in Spain today invites you to a memorable feast featuring her all-time favourite Spanish recipes. More than 170 tantalizing dishes, so that you can re-create the flavour of Spain in your own home.

Nord Riley's Spain

by Nord Riley. 272 pages

The best of popular columnist Nord Riley's writing over 14 years, brought together in the funniest book ever published about expatriate life in Spain. If you're not one of those lucky expats living in Nord Riley's Spain, by the time you've finished this book you'll wish you were.

Travellers in Spain

by David Mitchell. 192 pages (large format)

Spain through the eyes of famous travellers, from Richard Ford to Ernest Hemingway. This unique survey by David Mitchell, himself a respected observer of Spanish life, is a collection of the most outrageous, admiring, insulting, libellous, passionate, hilarious, thoughtful, bigoted, eloquent remarks ever made about any country. An invaluable key to understanding the Spanish character. Lavishly illustrated in colour and black and white. (Originally published as Here in Spain.)

A Selection of Wildflowers of Southern Spain

by Betty Molesworth Allen. 260 pages

Southern Spain is host to a rich variety of wildflowers in widely diverse habitats, some species growing nowhere else. This book describes more than 200 common plants of the region, each illustrated in full colour with simple text for easy identification and enjoyment.

You and the Law in Spain

by David Searl. 210 pages

Thousands of readers have relied on Lookout's best-selling You and the Law in Spain to guide them through the Spanish legal jungle. Now, author David Searl brings you a new, completely revised edition with even more information on taxes, work permits, cars, banking in Spain, buying property, Spain and the European Community, and lots more. It's a book no foreigner in Spain can afford to be without.

Inside Andalusia

by David Baird, 187 pages

A travel adventure through Spain's most fascinating region. David Baird invites you to explore an Andalusia you never dreamt of, to meet its people, and discover its exciting fiestas. Illustrated with brilliant colour photographs.

Spain's Wildlife

by Eric Robins. 182 pages

Illustrated by Spain's top nature photographer and written by Eric Robins, who has spent a decade studying the widlife of the Iberian peninsula, this book introduces you to some of Spain's rare and endangered species and tells you of their life-or-death struggle to survive.

On sale at bookstores in Spain, or by post from: Mirador Publications SL, Puebla Lucía, 29640 Fuengirola (Málaga) Spain

NOTES

NOTES

NOTES

NOTES

NOTES

NOTES